I0448388

July 2013

# ELDER JUSTICE

# More Federal Coordination and Public Awareness Needed

GAO-13-498

# ELDER JUSTICE

## More Federal Coordination and Public Awareness Needed

Highlights of GAO-13-498, a report to congressional requesters

## Why GAO Did This Study

As the percentage of older adults in the population increases, the number of older adults at risk of abuse also is growing. At the same time, constraints on public funds may limit assistance to the growing population of older adults in need. GAO was asked to review elder justice program issues. This report addresses: (1) the extent to which there is fragmentation, overlap, or duplication across the federal grant programs that support elder justice; (2) the extent to which federal programs coordinate their efforts and monitor elder justice outcomes; and (3) how state aging agencies, area agencies on aging, and service providers deliver federal elder justice services and what challenges, if any, they face in doing so. GAO reviewed relevant federal laws and regulations, identified federal elder justice programs, surveyed federal officials about program elements, reviewed program documentation, and visited agencies responsible for elder justice in Illinois, Virginia and Arizona. GAO selected states based on the percentage of the elderly in the state population, geographic dispersion, and percentage of the state's Older American Act funds devoted to elder care.

## What GAO Recommends

GAO recommends that HHS take the lead in identifying common objectives and outcomes for the federal elder justice effort and that HHS and Justice develop a national elder justice public awareness campaign. HHS concurred and Justice did not comment.

View GAO-13-498. For more information, contact Kay Brown at (202) 512-7215 or brownke@gao.gov

## What GAO Found

In fiscal year 2011, two agencies—the Departments of Health and Human Services (HHS) and Justice (Justice) —separately administered 12 fragmented but minimally overlapping programs that directed funds toward elder justice, with low risk of duplication. Specifically, because more than one federal agency administers these programs, GAO found that these grant programs are fragmented. Further, GAO found that overlap across the 12 programs was minimal because the programs varied with respect to (1) funding mechanisms and recipients, (2) elder abuse victims targeted, (3) service providers, and (4) activities conducted. For example, a few of these programs provided formula grants to all states and most dispersed discretionary grants to a limited number of recipients. Programs that supported victims of elder abuse generally assisted all types of victims, but some also focused on certain subgroups, such as older women. Some programs that assisted service providers also targeted specific subgroups, such as judges and court personnel. In addition, elder justice programs supported a wide range of activities. For example, one HHS program provided public education to help identify and prevent elder abuse, while a Justice program trained law enforcement officers to investigate instances of elder abuse. Considering the variation across funding mechanisms and recipients, the elder abuse victims and service providers targeted by the grants, and the types of activities conducted, overlap across the 12 programs is minimal and the risk of duplication—when two or more agencies or programs are engaged in the same activities or provide the same services to the same beneficiaries—is low.

We have previously reported that coordination is key to ensuring the efficient use of limited resources to address issues that cut across more than one agency. While federal coordination is in development—for example, HHS, Justice, and other agencies recently formed the Elder Justice Coordinating Council—federal agencies have yet to articulate common objectives and outcomes as precursors to future measures for elder justice programs, which would provide a rationale for coordination. Further, few federal programs tracked elder justice outcomes in 2011 or conducted program evaluations to assess effectiveness, making it difficult to determine what impact, if any, many programs have on victims of elder abuse.

Officials representing state aging agencies, area agencies on aging and service providers in the three states GAO visited identified the increased demand for elder justice services in a constrained fiscal environment as a major challenge in meeting the needs of the growing older adult population. Officials also cited the need for greater awareness of elder abuse by the public and training of direct service providers who interact with older adults on a regular basis, to help prevent elder abuse or recognize its symptoms. Five of the nine regional agency officials GAO spoke with said elder justice issues need to be elevated to national attention for the general public by a national public awareness campaign. The Elder Justice Coordinating Council is considering a recommendation to sponsor a national campaign but has not yet done so.

# Contents

## Figures

## Abbreviations

| | |
|---|---|
| ACL | Administration for Community Living |
| Advisory Board | Advisory Board on Elder Abuse |
| AoA | Administration on Aging |
| APS | Adult protective services |
| CFPB | Bureau of Consumer Financial Protection (commonly referred to as the Consumer Financial Protection Bureau) |
| Council | Elder Justice Coordinating Council |
| Working Group | Elder Justice Interagency Working Group |
| HHS | Department of Health and Human Services |
| HUD | Department of Housing and Urban Development |
| Justice | Department of Justice |
| EJA | Elder Justice Act of 2009 |
| EJCC | Elder Justice Coordinating Council |
| FTC | Federal Trade Commission |
| FinCEN | Financial Crimes Enforcement Network |
| NCEA | National Center on Elder Abuse |
| Office for Older Americans | Office for the Financial Protection of Older Americans |
| OAA | Older Americans Act of 1965 |
| SEC | Securities and Exchange Commission |
| Treasury | Department of the Treasury |
| VAWA | Violence Against Women Act of 1994 |

This is a work of the U.S. government and is not subject to copyright protection in the United States. The published product may be reproduced and distributed in its entirety without further permission from GAO. However, because this work may contain copyrighted images or other material, permission from the copyright holder may be necessary if you wish to reproduce this material separately.

July 10, 2013

The Honorable Lamar Alexander
Ranking Member
Committee on Health, Education, Labor and Pensions
United States Senate

The Honorable Michael B. Enzi
Ranking Member
Subcommittee on Children and Families
Committee on Health, Education, Labor and Pensions
United States Senate

The Honorable Bob Corker
United States Senate

Elder justice programs are designed to address the occurrence of elder abuse in American society and focus primarily on the prevention, identification, and response to elder abuse. At the same time that older adults comprise an increasing proportion of the nation's population, programs that provide assistance to this population may face fiscal constraints at the federal, state, and local level. We recently reported that federal leadership in the elder justice area is lacking and that a national strategy to address challenges related to elder financial exploitation in particular is needed.[1] These conditions and the expected growth in the number of older adults who may be at risk of abuse have raised questions in the Congress about the number and structure of federal programs with elder justice activities. You asked us to review federal elder justice program management issues. This report addresses (1) the extent to which there is fragmentation across the federal grant programs that support elder justice and the extent to which these grant programs overlap or support duplicative services; (2) the extent to which federal programs coordinate their efforts and monitor elder justice outcomes; and (3) how state aging agencies, area agencies on aging and service

---

[1]GAO, *Elder Justice: Stronger Federal Leadership Could Enhance National Response to Elder Abuse,* GAO-11-208 (Washington, D.C.: March 2, 2011) and *Elder Justice: National Strategy Needed to Effectively Combat Elder Financial Exploitation,* GAO-13-110 (Washington, D.C.: Nov. 15, 2012).

providers deliver federal elder justice services and what challenges, if any, they face in doing so.

Using the framework established in our prior work addressing fragmentation, overlap, and duplication, in this report we use the following definitions for analysis of elder justice programs:

- Fragmentation: when more than one federal agency (or more than one organization within an agency) is involved in the same broad area of national interest.
- Overlap: when programs have similar goals, devise similar strategies and activities to achieve those goals, or target similar users. Overlap may result from statutory or other limitations beyond an agency's control.
- Duplication: when two or more agencies or programs are engaged in the same activities or provide the same services to the same beneficiaries.[2]

To examine the extent to which fragmentation exists across the federal grant programs that support elder justice and the extent to which these grant programs overlap or support duplicative services, we developed an initial list of programs in federal agencies that met our definition of elder justice and one of three selection criteria: (1) programs that directed all funds toward elder justice activities; (2) programs that directed some funds toward elder justice activities, or (3) programs that supported elder justice as an allowable activity.[3] The third criterion pertains to programs that have a broader focus and target population than do elder justice programs, but may have some activities that relate to elder abuse, neglect or exploitation. In addition, programs had to have incurred obligations in fiscal year 2011 to be included in the list. Next, we surveyed federal agency officials to collect descriptive information about elder justice programs that met one of our first two selection criteria, or were determined to potentially meet one of those criteria but required additional

---

[2]GAO, *2012 Annual Report: Opportunities to Reduce Duplication, Overlap and Fragmentation, Achieve Savings, and Enhance Revenue*, GAO-12-342SP (Washington, D.C.: Feb. 28, 2012).

[3]While there is no standard definition for what constitutes a federal program, we defined "program" as an organized set of activities supported by a congressional appropriation, allocation, or authorization. This can include grants, initiatives, centers, loans, funds, and other types of assistance. Further, we defined a program as a single program even when its funds were allocated to other programs as well, such as a block grant.

information. The survey collected information on key program elements, including objectives, activities, target populations, outcome measures, and obligations during fiscal year 2011. The survey response rate was 100 percent. The survey also allowed us to confirm, exclude, and add programs based on consultations with agency officials. As a result of our analysis of the survey data and follow-up contact with agency officials, we identified 12 programs that met one of the first two selection criteria and funded elder justice activities in fiscal year 2011. We analyzed whether similarities and differences in key program elements indicated potential fragmentation, overlap, or duplication, and whether program officials monitored program outcomes. Appendix I provides a detailed description of our methodology for the survey and its limitations, as well as its scope.

To determine the extent to which federal programs coordinate their efforts and monitor elder justice outcomes, our survey collected information on federal elder justice programs' coordination, monitoring, and program evaluation. We conducted written follow-up with program officials about their efforts, reviewed their planning documents, and assessed this information to identify elder justice programs' monitoring and coordination efforts.

To determine how state aging agencies, area agencies on aging and service providers deliver federal elder justice services and what challenges, if any, they face in doing so, we conducted site visits to Arizona, Illinois, and Virginia. We selected these states because a relatively high percentage of the state population is over 60 years of age; geographic dispersion; and a relatively high percentage of Older Americans Act of 1965 funding in the state's budget is devoted to elder care.[4] In each state, we interviewed staff from the state aging agency, and three area aging agencies, and in one state, officials from two local service providers, about challenges in delivering elder justice services. We also interviewed experts in the field of aging and elder abuse including representatives of the American Bar Association-Commission on Law and Aging, the National Health Policy Forum, the National Association of States United for Aging and Disabilities, and the Woodrow Wilson International Center for Scholars. Findings from these site visits are not generalizable to all aging agencies or service providers, but provide important insights.

---

[4]Pub. L. No. 89-73, 79 Stat. 218 (codified as amended at 42 U.S.C. §§ 3001-3058ff).

We conducted this performance audit from March 2012 to July 2013 in accordance with generally accepted government auditing standards. Those standards require that we plan and perform the audit to obtain sufficient, appropriate evidence to provide a reasonable basis for our findings and conclusions based on the audit objectives. We believe that the evidence obtained provides a reasonable basis for our findings and conclusions based on our audit objectives

## Background

Elder justice can be defined as efforts to prevent, identify, and respond to elder abuse. The following are examples of the types of objectives federal elder justice programs may include:

- Preventing and identifying elder abuse, such as conducting outreach and public education and investigating allegations of elder abuse.
- Responding to elder abuse, such as providing counseling, prosecuting elder abuse cases, advocating on behalf of nursing home residents, and offering legal assistance.
- Providing training and technical assistance related to elder abuse for individuals and agencies.
- Conducting research related to elder abuse issues, such as the development of information and data systems and identifying the incidence.

## Federal Elder Justice Program Structure

Federal elder justice programs are administered and funded through a complex intergovernmental structure. The Older Americans Act of 1965 (OAA) established the Administration on Aging (AoA) within the Department of Health and Human Services (HHS) as the chief federal advocate for older Americans[5] and assigned responsibility for elder abuse prevention to the AoA. In April 2012, HHS established the Administration for Community Living (ACL), which brought together the AoA, the Office on Disability and the Administration on Developmental Disabilities to better align the federal programs that address the community living service and support needs of both the aging and disability populations, among other things.

---

[5]42 U.S.C. § 3012(a)(1).

Elder justice programs funded by HHS are implemented through the aging services network.[6] Authorized by the OAA, the aging services network was developed to help people age 60 and over maintain maximum independence in their homes and communities and to promote a continuum of care for vulnerable older adults. The aging services network is now made up of 56 state aging agencies, 629 area agencies on aging (AAAs), and almost 20,000 service provider organizations, many of which rely on volunteers, that deliver services to older adults.[7] Further, the OAA authorizes grants administered by the AoA, within ACL, to fund initiatives for those 60 years of age and older throughout the aging services network, including social services such as home-delivered meals, legal assistance, employment programs, research and community development projects, and training for professionals in the field of aging.[8] Elder justice programs supported by the Department of Justice (Justice) also are delivered through the aging services network as well as through other state agencies, local social service and government agencies, and tribal government agencies.

In order to be able to participate in OAA grants to states, the statute required states to establish AAAs to advocate for, plan, and coordinate programs for older persons, including elder justice programs.[9] AAAs provide services such as making elder abuse prevention presentations to local, and state organizations, training bank clerks and field workers such as sanitation, water department and utility employees to identify potential victims of elder abuse, and providing legal services. According to a report by the National Health Policy Forum, approximately 42 percent of AAAs are non-profit agencies, about 30 percent are part of city or county governments, and about 23 percent are part of councils of government or

---

[6]The OAA uses the term "aging network" (42 U.S.C. § 3002(5)) but we found the more descriptive term "aging services network" in widespread use.

[7] Area agencies on aging are sub-state organizations that can encompass one or more local governmental jurisdictions, such as cities and counties.

[8]42 U.S.C. § 3024.

[9]42 U.S.C. § 3025(a)(2)(A).

regional planning and development agencies.[10] The rest are located in colleges, community action agencies and other organizations.

State Adult Protective Services (APS) programs also provide services to abused, neglected or exploited older adults and adults with disabilities. The abuse can be physical, psychological, or sexual, and the exploitation can involve either financial or material possessions. Neglect can be inattention by a caregiver or the inability of an individual to care for themselves. APS programs are primarily the responsibility of states and APS programs vary greatly with regard to the age ranges they serve, and how cases are handled. States tend to fund APS programs through multiple funding sources, including the federal Social Services Block Grant.[11]

States are primarily responsible for protecting older adults from abuse. However, the OAA and a number of other federal laws include provisions that can address elder justice in support of state and local efforts, including the following:

- The Elder Justice Act of 2009 recognizes an older adult's rights and his or her ability to be free of abuse, neglect, and exploitation.[12] The Act includes provisions to address some of the limitations of federal and state efforts to prevent and respond to abuse, neglect, and exploitation of older adults, including a new state formula grant program under Title XX of the Social Security Act for adult protective services, requirements for reporting crimes in long-term care facilities, and the development of advisory bodies on elder abuse.
- The Tax Relief and Health Care Act of 2006[13] authorizes HHS to study the feasibility of establishing a uniform national database on elder abuse. Even though funding for the data base has not been authorized, HHS completed the feasibility study in March

---

[10]National Health Policy Forum Background Paper No. 83: The Aging Services Network: Serving a Vulnerable and Growing Elderly Population in Tough Economic Times, December 13, 2011.

[11]42 U.S.C. §§ 1397-1397k-3.

[12]Pub. L. No.111-148, tit. VI, subtit. H, §§ 6701-6703, 124 Stat. 119, 782-804 (2010) (codified at 42 U.S.C. §§ 1397j-1397m-5).

[13]Pub. L. No. 109-432, § 405, 120 Stat. 2922, 3053.

2010.The study recommended three options for constructing a national data base on elder abuse from existing administrative data collection systems.

- The Victims of Trafficking and Violence Protection Act of 2000,[14] which amended the Violence Against Women Act of 1994 (VAWA),[15] authorized several domestic violence programs, including training for prosecutors and other relevant court officers about dealing with elder abuse, neglect, and exploitation.The Violence Against Women and Department of Justice Reauthorization Act of 2005[16] amended VAWA to authorize grants for programs to assist victims of elder abuse, neglect, and exploitation, aged 50 and older. The activities funded included training programs for law enforcement, prosecutors, government agency officials, victim assistants, and others in recognizing and addressing elder abuse and exploitation; providing services for victims of violence; supporting collaborative community responses to victims; and conducting cross-training for victim service organizations. The VAWA was reauthorized in February 2013.[17]

The focus of HHS's elder justice programs is on social services for older adults, and Justice supports elder justice programs and activities that include civil and criminal prosecutions of elder abuse and neglect as well as health care fraud cases. Justice also helps fund state and local efforts to reduce and prevent victimization of older individuals and to support services for older victims. These efforts address several types of abuse, and exploitation, including domestic violence, sexual assault, and consumer fraud. Several other federal agencies, including the Federal Trade Commission, the Department of Housing and Urban Development, the Securities and Exchange Commission, and the Consumer Financial Protection Bureau (CFPB) also provide support for elder justice programs in areas related to financial and consumer protection.[18] Combating elder

---

[14]Pub. L. No. 106-386, sec.1209(a), § 40802, 114 Stat. 1464, 1508 (codified at 42 U.S.C. § 14041a).

[15]Pub. L. No. 103-322, tit. IV, 108 Stat. 1796, 1902-1955.

[16]Pub. L. No. 109-162, § 205, 119 Stat. 2960, 3002 (codified as amended at 42 U.S.C. § 14041a).

[17]Violence Against Women Reauthorization Act of 2013, Pub. L. No. 113-4, 127 Stat. 54.

[18]See appendix II, table 9.

GAO-13-498 Elder Justice Programs

financial abuse is explicitly included in the mission of the CFPB's recently established Office of Financial Protection for Older Americans.[19] Figure 1 shows the federal, state, regional and local service agencies that support and deliver elder justice efforts.

---

[19]12 U.S.C. § 5493(g)(3).

**Figure 1: Agencies and Other Individuals Positioned to Support Elder Justice Efforts[a]**

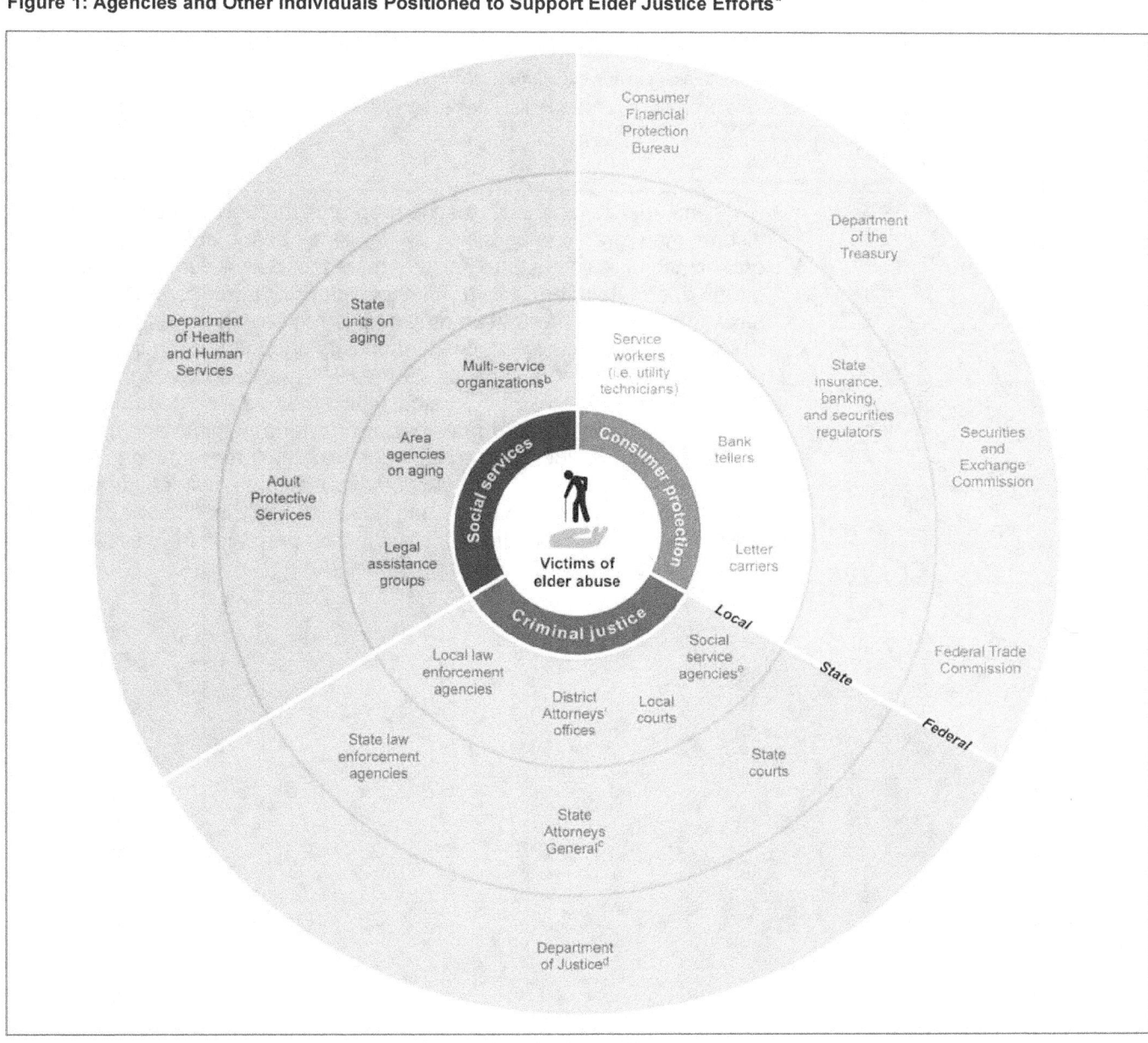

Source: GAO analysis of information provided by agencies.

[a]The relationship between the federal and the state and local agencies in a given system varies.

b Multiservice organizations are organizations that deliver more than one type of public benefit program, such as congregate meals, Supplemental Nutrition Assistance Program cards, and legal assistance.

c State attorneys general may also play a consumer protection role.

d Justice also plays a consumer protection role.

e Social service agencies include domestic violence and sexual assault victim services providers.

## Elder Justice Funding

HHS and Justice fund elder justice programs through formula grants and discretionary grants to agencies as well as tribal and non-profit organizations in each state. For programs that deliver funds through grants, the state agencies submit applications or agree to meet certain requirements with information provided by regional or local agencies, which may provide the services themselves or contract with independent providers to deliver the services. Some HHS and Justice programs are funded through discretionary grants, which may be awarded directly to any eligible applicant that meets eligibility criteria. Eligible applicants for HHS and Justice elder justice discretionary grant programs may include area agencies on aging, multi-service organizations, district attorneys' offices, legal assistance groups and postsecondary institutions.[20] Figure 2 illustrates the flow of funding for elder justice programs from HHS and Justice to several types of grant recipients.

[20] The National Institute on Aging and the National Center on Elder Abuse provide funding via federal grants to postsecondary institutions. 42 U.S.C. §§ 285e and 3012(d).

**Figure 2: Formula Grant and Discretionary Grant Elder Justice Funding**

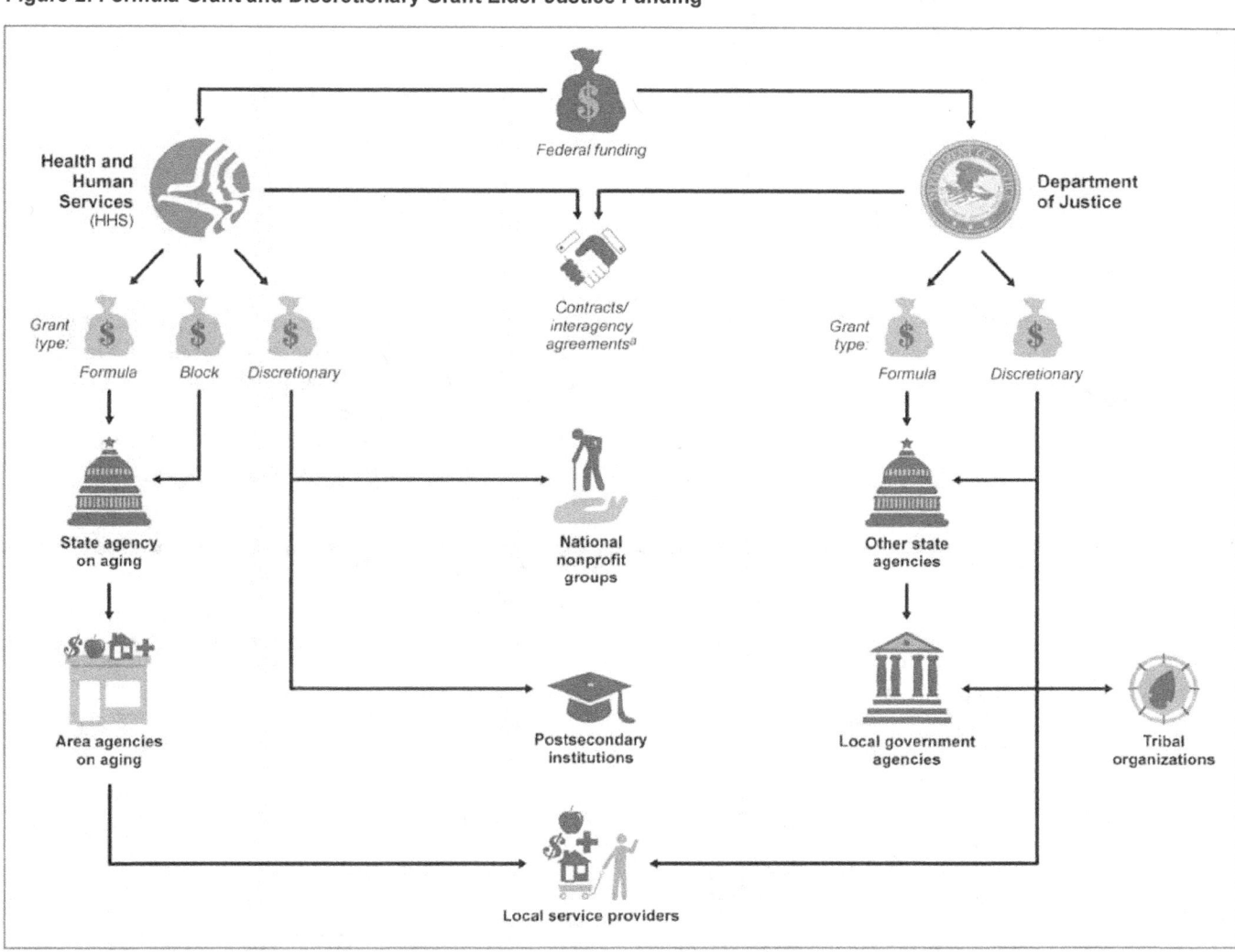

Source: GAO analysis of survey data and program documentation.

[a]HHS and Justice administer elder justice programs that did not award grants but rather used funds to conduct activities and administered contracts and interagency agreements as appropriate.

# Federal Elder Justice Programs Are Fragmented but Minimally Overlapping, Reducing the Risk for Duplication

## Federal Elder Justice Programs Are Administered by Multiple Agencies

In fiscal year 2011, HHS and Justice administered 12 programs that directed federal funds toward elder justice programs. Seven of these programs directed all funds toward elder justice in fiscal year 2011; the other five directed some of their funds toward elder justice but supported activities for other purposes, as well. Table 1 lists the 12 programs that directed funds toward elder justice. The fiscal year 2011 obligations reported in table 1 include federal funds only.

**Table 1: Federal Programs That Directed All or Some Funds toward Elder Justice in Fiscal Year 2011**

| Program | Directed all funds toward elder justice | Directed some funds toward elder justice | Fiscal year 2011 federal obligations |
|---|---|---|---|
| Health and Human Services programs | | | |
| Prevention of Elder Abuse, Neglect, and Exploitation | X | | $5,033,000 |
| Long-Term Care (LTC) Ombudsman Program | | X | [a] |
| National Center on Elder Abuse | X | | $804,000 |
| National Adult Protective Services (APS) Resource Center[b] | X | | $200,000 |
| National Long-Term Care Ombudsman Resource Center | | X | [a] |
| National Institute on Aging (NIA) Research Activities Related to Elder Mistreatment | X | | $1,134,000 |
| Interpersonal Violence within Families and Among Acquaintances Prevention | | X | [a] |
| Justice programs | | | |
| Services, Training, Officers, and Prosecutors (STOP) Violence Against Women Formula Grant Program | | X | [a] |
| Enhanced Training and Services to End Violence Against and Abuse of Women Later in Life Program | X | | $5,249,000 |
| Coordinated Tribal Assistance Solicitations: Tribal Elder Outreach Program | X | | $1,454,000 |

| Program | Directed all funds toward elder justice | Directed some funds toward elder justice | Fiscal year 2011 federal obligations |
|---|---|---|---|
| Grants to Encourage Arrest Policies and Enforcement of Protection Orders Program | | X | [a] |
| Elder Justice and Nursing Home Initiative | X | | $747,000 |

Source: GAO analysis of survey data and agency documents.

[a]Programs that directed some funds toward elder justice were not able to report obligations specifically for elder justice because those activities are not tracked separately from overall program activities, according to officials.

[b]The federal government provides technical assistance and support to states for APS through this resource center. APS efforts are primarily the responsibility of states and there have been no significant federal funds provided specifically and solely for APS.

Because more than one agency is involved in this same broad area of national interest, and the agencies have just begun to coordinate their activities, these programs are fragmented. However, the administration has begun to take steps to enhance coordination which, as we previously reported, can help address some of the problems that arise from a fragmented array of programs supporting the same national interest.[21]

In addition, we identified 34 other federal programs that supported elder justice indirectly—by providing federal funds for elder justice as an allowable activity(see fig. 3). Because elder justice was an allowable activity in these 34 programs, grant recipients determined whether elder justice activities would be conducted in a given fiscal year.[22] As a result, federal program managers could not tell us which elder justice activities to compare for that year, to determine if overlap or duplication occurred, for those 34 grant programs.

[21]GAO, *Results-Oriented Government: Practices that Can Help Enhance and Sustain Collaboration among Federal Agencies*, GAO-06-15 (Washington, D.C.: Oct. 21, 2005), and GAO-12-342SP.

[22] See appendix II for more information on 34 programs.

## Figure 3: Number of Federal Elder Justice Programs and Administering Departments and Agencies

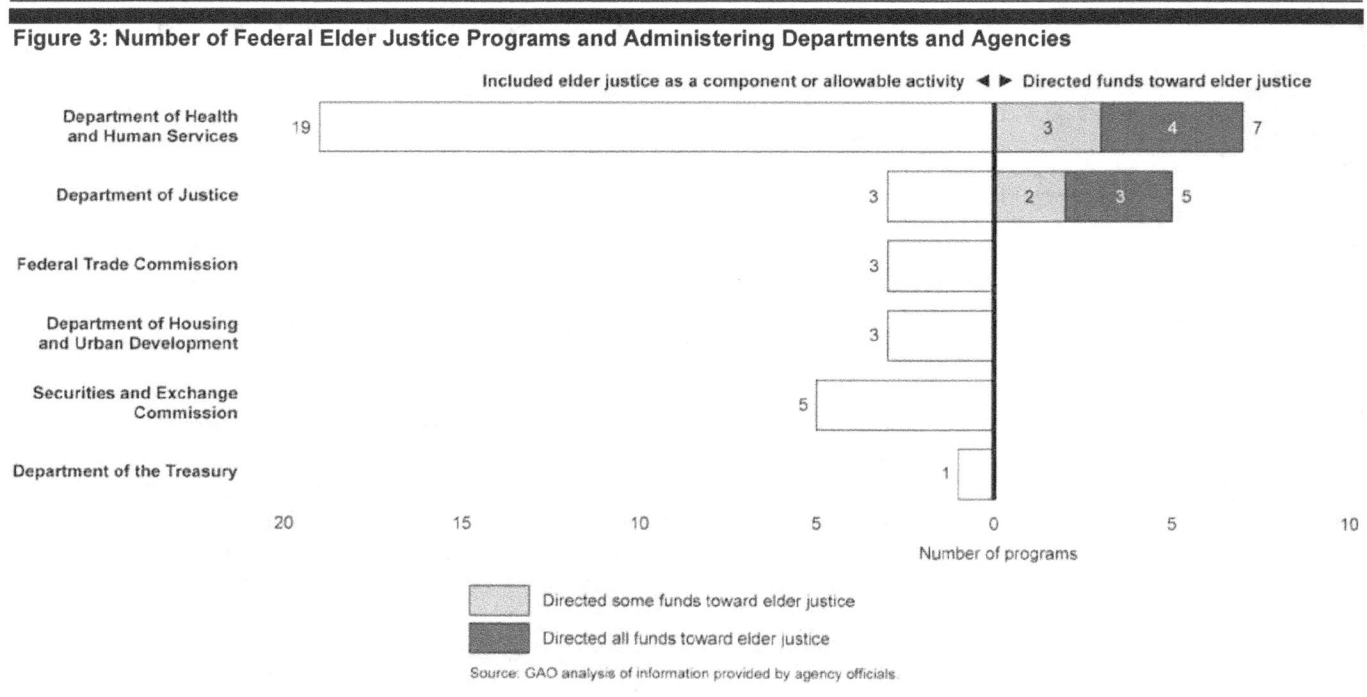

Included elder justice as a component or allowable activity ◄ ► Directed funds toward elder justice

| | | |
|---|---|---|
| Department of Health and Human Services | 19 | 3 | 4 | 7 |
| Department of Justice | 3 | 2 | 3 | 5 |
| Federal Trade Commission | 3 | |
| Department of Housing and Urban Development | 3 | |
| Securities and Exchange Commission | 5 | |
| Department of the Treasury | 1 | |

Number of programs

☐ Directed some funds toward elder justice
■ Directed all funds toward elder justice

Source: GAO analysis of information provided by agency officials.

## Overlap and Duplication are Minimal in Federal Elder Justice Effort

The 12 programs supported elder justice activities through a variety of federal funding mechanisms. Ten of the programs supported the federal elder justice effort through grants to a variety of grantees such as states, localities, universities, and other grantees, while the remaining two programs—HHS' Interpersonal Violence within Families and Among Acquaintances Prevention program and Justice's Elder Justice and Nursing Home Initiative—did not award grants but administered contracts and interagency agreements. Because few of these programs provided formula grants to all states and most dispersed discretionary grants to limited number of recipients of several types, there is minimal overlap in this area.

Specifically, 3 of the 10 grant programs provided a guaranteed base of funding through formula grants to all states; however, each of these programs awarded grants to state agencies for different purposes and the state agency recipients of the HHS grants differed from the recipients of the Justice grant.[23] One HHS program awarded formula grants to state aging agencies to fund elder justice prevention and awareness activities and the other program funded assistance to residents of long term care facilities. The Justice program awarded formula grants to state criminal justice agencies to fund elder justice activities as well as other law enforcement and prosecution strategies. Moreover, 7 of the 10 elder justice grant programs required recipients to compete for funding by awarding discretionary grants to a limited number of grant recipients. Three of these discretionary grants provided funding to direct service providers, such as local organizations serving domestic and sexual assault victims, local governments, or courts. The remaining four discretionary grants provided funding to a nonprofit organization and a limited number of postsecondary institutions to operate resource centers for state and local governments or to conduct research related to elder mistreatment.

Federal elder justice programs also provided support for a variety of types of victims and potential victims of elder abuse. Nine of the 12 programs provided services to victims and potential victims of elder abuse: 5 provided assistance to all types of victims and 4 focused on key subgroups of victims, further reducing the potential for overlap. For example, 1 of the 4 programs served older female victims, another targeted victims in long-term care facilities, and still another served victims in tribal communities. Table 2 displays the types of victims targeted by the federal elder justice programs we identified.

---

[23]The three formula grant programs were HHS' Prevention of Elder Abuse, Neglect, and Exploitation program (42 U.S.C. § 3058), HHS' Long-Term Care (LTC) Ombudsman Program (42 U.S.C. § 3058g), and Justice's Services, Training, Officer, and Prosecutors (STOP) Violence Against Women Formula Grant Program (42 U.S.C. § 3796gg-1).

**Table 2: Variation in Types of Victims Targeted under Federal Elder Justice Programs**

| Program name | Subgroups of victims | | | | |
| --- | --- | --- | --- | --- | --- |
| | All types of older adult victims | Female victims of all ages[c] | Older female victims[c] | Victims in LTC facilities | Victims in tribal communities[c] |
| Health and Human Services programs | | | | | |
| Prevention of Elder Abuse, Neglect, and Exploitation | X | | | | |
| Long-Term Care (LTC) Ombudsman Program | | | | X | |
| National Center on Elder Abuse | X | | | | |
| National Adult Protective Services (APS) Resource Center | a | | | | |
| National Long-Term Care Ombudsman Resource Center | a | | | | |
| National Institute on Aging (NIA) Research Activities Related to Elder Mistreatment | a | | | | |
| Interpersonal Violence within Families and Among Acquaintances Prevention[b] | X | | | | |
| Justice programs | | | | | |
| Services, Training, Officers, Prosecutors (STOP) Violence Against Women Formula Grant Program | | X | | | |
| Enhanced Training and Services to End Violence Against and Abuse of Women Later in Life Program[d] | | | X | | |
| Coordinated Tribal Assistance Solicitations: Tribal Elder Outreach Program | | | | | X |
| Grants to Encourage Arrest Policies and Enforcement of Protection Orders Program | X | | | | |
| Elder Justice and Nursing Home Initiative[b] | X | | | | |

Source: GAO analysis of survey data and agency documents.

[a] These programs did not directly serve victims or potential victims directly, rather they engaged in research on elder abuse in general.

[b] These programs did not award grants but rather used funds to conduct activities and administered contracts and interagency agreements as appropriate.

[c] Subgroup name includes "potential victims".

[d] Program officials reported that this program also serves some male victims.

Moreover, a variety of service providers—organizations that deliver services at the state and local level—were supported by the 12 elder justice programs. In 2011, 8 programs targeted specific subgroups of service providers while 4 programs did not target subgroups of service providers. Even some of the 4 programs that provided support to all types of service providers specialized to some degree. For example, one program supported outreach focused on tribal elders while another focused on elder mistreatment research (see table 3).

**Table 3: Variation in Types of Service Providers Supported by Federal Elder Justice Programs**

| Subgroups of service providers | All types of service providers | Legal and law enforcement professionals | Medical/health care professionals | State/local APS workers | State/local LTC providers | LTC facilities workers |
|---|---|---|---|---|---|---|
| **Program name** | | | | | | |
| **Health and Human Services programs** | | | | | | |
| Prevention of Elder Abuse, Neglect, and Exploitation | X | | | | | |
| Long-Term Care (LTC) Ombudsman Program | X | | | | X | X |
| National Center on Elder Abuse | X | | | | | |
| National Adult Protective Services (APS) Resource Center | | | | X | | |
| National Long-Term Care Ombudsman Resource Center | | | | | X | |
| National Institute on Aging (NIA) Research Activities Related to Elder Mistreatment | X | | | | | |
| Interpersonal Violence within Families and Among Acquaintances Prevention[a] | X | | X | X | | |
| **Justice programs** | | | | | | |
| Services, Training, Officers, Prosecutors (STOP) Violence Against Women Formula Grant Program | X | X | X | | | |
| Enhanced Training and Services to End Violence Against and Abuse of Women Later in Life Program | X | X | | | | |
| Coordinated Tribal Assistance Solicitations: Tribal Elder Outreach Program | X | | | | | |
| Grants to Encourage Arrest Policies and Enforcement of Protection Orders Program | | X | | | | |
| Elder Justice and Nursing Home Initiative[a] | X | X | X | | | |

Source: GAO analysis of survey data and agency documents.

[a]These programs did not award grants but rather used funds to conduct activities at the federal level and administered contracts and interagency agreements as appropriate. In addition to supporting all types of service providers, such as providing information and training to professionals who work with older adults, these programs targeted specific subgroups of service providers, such as medical and health care professionals.

In addition to serving a range of elder abuse victims and service providers, the 12 programs we identified varied with respect to the activities they supported, with minimal overlap in some activities (see table 4). For example, 4 programs provided victim assistance services. Two programs provided support for conducting investigations of complaints concerning different members of the older adult community, including residents of long-term care facilities and female victims in the community.

# Table 4: Variation in Activities Supported by Federal Programs that Directed Funds toward Elder Justice

| Program | Victim assistance services | Investigations | Law enforcement and prosecution of cases | Education, outreach, and information dissemination | Training and technical assistance | Advisory services and guidance | Information and data management | Promote state/local coordination | Developing policies, programs, protocols, and procedures | Research |
|---|---|---|---|---|---|---|---|---|---|---|
| Health and Human Services programs | | | | | | | | | | |
| Prevention of Elder Abuse, Neglect, and Exploitation[a] | | | | X | X | X | | X | | X |
| Long-Term Care (LTC) Ombudsman Program | | X | | | X | X | | | | |
| National Center on Elder Abuse | | | | X | X | X | | | | X |
| National Adult Protective Services (APS) Resource Center | | | | X | X | | | | | X |
| National Long-Term Care Ombudsman Resource Center | | | | X | X | X | | X | | |
| National Institute on Aging Research Activities Related to Elder Mistreatment | | | | | | | | | | X |
| Interpersonal Violence within Families and Among Acquaintances Prevention[b] | | | | X | X | X | | | | |

| Program | Victim assistance services | Investigations | Law enforcement and prosecution of cases | Education, outreach, and information dissemination | Training and technical assistance | Advisory services and guidance | Information and data management | Promote state/ local coordination | Developing policies, programs, protocols, and procedures | Research |
|---|---|---|---|---|---|---|---|---|---|---|
| Justice programs | | | | | | | | | | |
| Services, Training, Officers, Prosecutors (STOP) Violence Against Women Formula Grant Program[a] | X | X | X | X | X | | X | X | X | |
| Enhanced Training and Services to End Violence Against and Abuse of Women Later in Life Program[a] | X | | | X | X | | | X | | |
| Coordinated Tribal Assistance Solicitations: Tribal Elder Outreach Program[a] | X | | | X | | | | X | | |
| Grants to Encourage Arrest Policies and Enforcement of Protection Orders Progam[a] | X | | | X | X | | X | X | X | |
| Elder Jus ice and Nursing Home Ini iative[b] | | | X | | X | | | X | | |

Source: GAO analysis of survey data and agency documents.

[a]For these programs the granting agency (HHS or Justice) identifies a range of activities grantees may conduct, though grantees are not required to conduct them all. As a result, some grantees may not engage in each of the activities identified here.

[b]These programs did not award grants but rather used funds to conduct activities at the federal level and administered contracts and interagency agreements as appropriate.

Three broad categories of activity—education, outreach, and information dissemination; training and technical assistance to service providers; and promoting state and local coordination—were supported by most of the 12 programs we identified. While some of these activities—education and outreach training for service providers, and state and local coordination—appear to overlap, these activities were not necessarily providing similar services to similar populations. For example, one program supported public education and outreach to potential victims to promote financial literacy among older adults and prevent financial exploitation. Another program trained law enforcement officers to recognize and investigate instances of abuse and trained staff in victim services organizations and governmental agencies to understand the role each plays in addressing elder abuse in the community. A third program promoted local coordination among human services organizations, law enforcement, and community development programs just within tribal communities. Further, some of the grant programs identify several allowable activities grantees may conduct using program funds, only a few of which may be elder justice-related, but do not require grantees to conduct all of them. In one case, the sponsoring agency does not track which elder justice projects are funded. For example, in describing the department's grant administration practices for the STOP Violence program, a Justice official explained that state agencies maintain records of the elder justice projects they fund but Justice does not. Thus, the number of grantees that conduct elder justice activities is not known by Justice.

When considering, collectively, the variation in the types of funding mechanisms and grant recipients, the elder abuse victims and service providers targeted by the grants, and the types of activities conducted, we found overlap across the 12 programs was minimal. In addition, the potentially overlapping activities have been cited as being in need of greater federal emphasis, as we will discuss later in this report. For example, public awareness and training for professionals working with elder abuse victims were two of the areas identified by some of the state and local officials we interviewed as those in which increased federal support would be beneficial. Also, previously discussed, we have recommended that coordination among state and local organizations has helped mitigate the effects of increasingly limited resources.

Moreover, the key differences noted above, in conjunction with low levels of funding, reduce the risk that two or more area agencies on aging or local service providers would be providing the same services to the same beneficiaries—that is, that they are providing duplicative services. With respect to low funding levels, by the time federal elder justice funds are obligated to grantees nationwide, the amount of funds available to any individual service provider is likely to be low. State officials in all three states we visited said that HHS is the primary federal funding source for their elder justice activities. Under two HHS programs, the Prevention of Elder Abuse, Neglect, and Exploitation program and the Long-Term Care (LTC) Ombudsman Program, the federal government distributes funds to state aging agencies, which then allocate funds to area agencies on aging or local service providers. For example, in fiscal year 2011, of the $5,033,000 total obligations for the Prevention of Elder Abuse, Neglect and Exploitation program, which directs all funds toward elder justice, HHS provided $197,380 to Illinois' state aging agency. The allocation to one of the state's 13 area agencies on aging was $14,488, which it then distributed to numerous other local service providers working directly with older adults, such as county human service agencies. In Virginia, HHS provided $118,040 to the state aging agency from the Prevention of Elder Abuse, Neglect and Exploitation program fiscal year 2011 obligations. According to officials at one of Virginia's 25 area agencies on aging, the allocation to that agency was $3,027 for that fiscal year.

# Federal Coordination of Elder Justice Activities Is in Development, but Monitoring Is Limited

## Federal Coordination of Elder Justice Activities Is in Development

We have previously reported that coordination is key to ensuring the efficient use of limited resources to address issues that cut across more than one agency.[24] With two key federal agencies, HHS and Justice, involved in elder justice, and the range of activities and individuals served under their programs, coordination may help ensure the federal elder justice effort draws on their respective expertise and mitigates the effects of fragmentation, as we have also reported.[25] In addition, we have

---

[24]GAO, *Results-Oriented Government: Practices that Can Help Enhance and Sustain Collaboration among Federal Agencies,* GAO-06-15 (Washington, D.C.: Oct. 21, 2005).

[25] GAO-06-15.

identified practices that can enhance coordination efforts, such as defining and articulating a common federal outcome or purpose agencies are seeking to achieve, consistent with their respective goals and missions. Developing a common federal outcome establishes a rationale for agencies to collaborate that helps overcome significant differences in agencies' missions, cultures, and established ways of doing business that may lead them to work at cross purposes.

HHS and Justice are involved in developing efforts to coordinate their elder justice activities. Most recently, the Elder Justice Coordinating Council (Council) was established under the Elder Justice Act of 2009 (EJA) to address cross-agency coordination of activities relating to elder abuse, neglect, and exploitation.[26] According to the EJA, the Council should include members representing HHS, Justice, and other federal entities with responsibilities or programs related to elder abuse. The Council held an inaugural meeting in October 2012, where it identified four issue areas for action—financial exploitation, public policy and awareness, enhancing response, and advancing research—and collected white papers from issue area experts. The white papers included recommendations for improving and advancing the field of elder justice. The Council is required to make recommendations to the Secretary of HHS for the coordination of elder justice activities by relevant federal agencies and report to Congress on accomplishments, challenges, and recommendations for legislative action every 2 years.

The Council met again in May 2013 to consider next steps. The Elder Justice Interagency Working Group (Working Group), an informal group designed to bring together federal officials responsible for carrying out elder justice activities, presented recommendations distilled from the white papers.[27] The working group's recommendations included such actions as launching an elder justice web site, developing elder justice forensic centers, a national APS data system, a national public awareness campaign, and strategies for combating financial exploitation in collaboration with industry.

---

[26] 42 U.S.C. § 1397k.

[27] Federal agencies participating in the Working Group include HHS, Justice, the CFPB, the Social Security Administration, the United States Postal Inspection Service, Housing and Urban Development, the Department of the Treasury, the Federal Trade Commission, and the Securities and Exchange Commission.

The EJA also established an Advisory Board on Elder Abuse, Neglect, and Exploitation (Advisory Board), which has a mission, distinct from the Council, of developing innovative approaches to improving the quality of long-term care, including preventing abuse, neglect, and exploitation.[28] The Advisory Board is tasked with creating short- and long-term strategic plans for the development of the elder justice field and making recommendations to the Council. Unlike the Council, which is comprised of federal agency officials who administer elder justice programs, the Advisory Board will be made up of appointed members from the general public with experience and expertise in elder abuse, neglect, and exploitation prevention, detection, treatment, intervention, and prosecution. Progress so far has included a solicitation for nominations for members, issued by HHS on July14, 2010.[29]

In addition, HHS and Justice officials from 10 of the 12 elder justice programs we identified said they were involved in informal or ad hoc coordination efforts with other federal programs. For example, officials representing 8 programs reported participating in joint program planning and implementation, such as assisting in the review of grant solicitations, collecting and sharing materials to support elder mistreatment prosecutions, and supporting training initiatives. Other coordination efforts program officials reported include participating in joint information sessions—such as elder abuse awareness events—jointly funding a training initiative, and sharing data and information about trends, prevention efforts, and responses to abuse, with other agencies or programs.

## Federal Programs Did Not Track Elder Justice Outcomes in 2011

While federal agencies have taken steps to better coordinate their efforts, less progress has been made in articulating and tracking common goals for federal elder justice activities. Program officials reported that 4 of the 12 federal programs we identified tracked elder justice outcomes in 2011 and one had conducted a program evaluation to determine effectiveness.

We have previously reported that agency-wide strategic planning practices required under the Government Performance and Results Act of

---

[28]42 U.S.C.§1397k-1.

[29]Establishment of the Advisory Board on Elder Abuse, Neglect, and Exploitation,75 Fed. Reg. 40,838 (July 14, 2010).

1993 (GPRA)[30]—as recently enhanced by the GPRA Modernization Act of 2010[31]—can also serve as leading practices for planning at lower organizational levels, such as individual programs or initiatives.[32] GPRA provides federal agencies with a way to focus on results and improve agency performance by, among other things, developing strategic plans. Examples of strategic plan components include a mission statement; general goals and objectives, including outcome-oriented goals; and a description of how the goals and objectives are to be achieved.

While HHS and Justice, the two agencies that oversee the 12 federal elder justice programs we identified, each have defined broad strategic goals and objectives at the department level that may impact elder justice (see table 5), and ACL has identified a strategic goal related to its elder justice responsibilities, the departments have not formally defined common goals for addressing concerns of elder abuse, neglect, and exploitation.

---

[30]Pub. L. No. 103-62, § 4(b), 107 Stat. 285, 287 (codified as amended at 31 U.S.C. § 1115(a)(1)).

[31]Pub. L. No. 111-352, § 3, 124 Stat. 3866, 3867-68 (2011) (codified at 31 U.S.C. § 1115(a)(1)).

[32]GAO, *Veteran-Owned Small Businesses: Planning and Data System for VA's Verification Program Need Improvement*, GAO-13-95 (Washington, D.C.: January 14, 2013).

**Table 5: Strategic Goals and Objectives under HHS and Justice That May Address Elder Justice**

| Department-level strategic goal[a] | Related objective | Agency-level goal specific to elder justice[a] |
|---|---|---|
| **Health and Human Services** | | |
| • Strategic goal 3: Advance the health, safety, and well-being of the American people. | • Objective 3.C: Improve the accessibility and quality of supportive services for people with disabilities and older adults. | • Administration for Community Living strategic goal 4: Ensure the rights of older people and prevent their abuse, neglect, and exploitation. |
| **Justice** | | |
| • Strategic goal 2: Prevent crime, protect the rights of the American people, and enforce federal law.[b]<br><br>• Strategic goal 3: Ensure and support the fair, impartial, efficient, and transparent administration of justice at the federal, state, local, tribal, and international levels. | • Objective 2.2: Prevent and intervene in crimes against vulnerable populations; uphold the rights of, and improve services to, America's crime victims.<br><br>• Objective 3.1: Promote and strengthen relationships and strategies for the administration of justice with state, local, tribal, and international law enforcement. | • None identified[c] |

Source: GAO analysis of agency documents.

[a] For our reporting purposes, "department-level" refers to goals set at the level of the Department of Health and Human Services and the Department of Justice. "Agency-level" refers to goals set at sub-department levels, such as the Administration on Aging at HHS or the Office on Violence Against Women at Justice.

[b] Justice's fiscal year 2012 performance and accountability report also cites priority goals, intended to represent critical elements of the agency's strategic plan, which includes a priority goal to protect those most in need of help, such as vulnerable populations including the elderly.

[c] While not defined as a strategic goal, Justice's Office on Violence Against Women (OVW) identified a 'priority area' in its fiscal year 2013 budget submission to Congress for extending OVW programming to underserved communities, including elderly women.

Among the 12 federal programs, we determined that 4 tracked outcomes for potential victims of elder justice in 2011.

• HHS's LTC Ombudsman Program reported the number of complaints made by residents in long-term care facilities, which include those related to elder abuse, neglect, or exploitation, that were resolved to the satisfaction of the resident.

• HHS's NIA Developmental Research on Elder Mistreatment program tracked the number of scientific publications resulting from NIA funding as a measure of the program's performance in meeting its intended purpose of supporting research on elder mistreatment.

- Justice's Tribal Elder Outreach Program[33] monitored outcomes related to service delivery for individual grant recipients, though these data were not aggregated for the full program. Outcomes individual grantees reported included the number of tribal victims served as a result of outreach efforts, according to Justice officials.
- Justice's Abuse in Later Life Program monitored outcomes at the grantee level. Outcomes the program tracked included the number of professionals trained to respond to domestic violence and sexual assault as well as the number of individuals receiving services.[34]

For three of the eight programs that did not track elder justice outcomes in 2011, officials said they plan to do so in the future. For example, officials from two of the programs that directed all funds toward elder justice said they plan to develop and monitor outcomes. For example, HHS's National APS Resource Center has identified program outputs, that will inform the development of outcome measures, such as a literature review of evidence-based APS programs and a related webinar, which will aim to improve the knowledge-base of participants. Similarly, the National Center on Elder Abuse,[35] also funded by HHS, has identified outcomes such as elder abuse awareness and the extent to which research findings are integrated into training and practice.

Similarly, formal evaluation of federal elder justice programs is limited. As we have previously reported, researchers designing formal evaluations for other programs, including one welfare program, have found that they had to fit the evaluation design to available time and resources, even when an evaluation is planned for the state rather than the federal level.[36] For example, in some cases, conducting an evaluation for an entire state may be determined to be so expensive that data collection has to be limited to a portion of the state. Thus, individual program efforts may not always be feasible within the resources of many elder justice programs. Nevertheless, one program, HHS' NIA research program, held a conference to evaluate the progress of research supported by grants

---

[33] 42 U.S.C. § 10603(c)(1).

[34] 42 U.S.C. § 14041a.

[35] 42 U.S.C. § 3012(d).

[36] GAO, *Designing Evaluations: 2012 Revision*, GAO-12-208G (Washington, D.C.: Jan. 31, 2012); and *Welfare Reform: Data Available to Assess TANF's Progress*, GAO-01-298 (Washington, D.C.: Feb. 28, 2001).

awarded to research elder justice issues in 2010. Three of the 11 remaining programs also indicated they plan to conduct evaluations in the future once more work has been completed or if funding becomes available. Officials from the other 8 programs reported they have not recently conducted nor do they plan to conduct a formal evaluation that includes an assessment of elder justice activities. Program officials cited several factors that limit their ability to formally evaluate their programs, including variability of program activities and scope year by year, insufficient data due to a short period of implementation for newer programs, and limited resources, including funding devoted to and expertise in program evaluation.

Given the costs associated with evaluating individual programs, developing common objectives and outcomes for HHS and Justice elder justice programs could be a first step in assessing the federal effort. As noted, coordination of these programs is just under way and HHS and Justice have not developed common objectives for the elder justice effort nor have they defined a set of common outcomes, which are necessary precursors to future performance measures, that could be used to evaluate the federal effort as a whole. Without progress on these fronts, the federal government cannot assess the effectiveness of its effort nor the efficient use of resources devoted to elder justice activities.

# Challenges Persist in Serving Older Adults and Stakeholders Identified a Need for Additional Training and Awareness

Officials from the state aging agencies, area agencies on aging, and service providers we interviewed identified the increased demand for services in a constrained fiscal environment as a major challenge in meeting the needs of the growing older adult population. State aging agency, area agency on aging, and service provider officials also cited the need for greater awareness of elder abuse, by both the public and individuals who interact with older adults, to help prevent elder abuse or recognize its symptoms. Further, officials in all of the state aging agencies we contacted told us that elder abuse cases are increasing, especially financial exploitation cases. For example, one state official we spoke with said that, as they gave greater emphasis to such cases, they found that elder justice cases involving financial exploitation, in particular, take longer to investigate, use financial records that are difficult to obtain, and are often harder to prove than physical or emotional abuse.

Elder justice activities are a small but important component of the broad range of services area agencies on aging (AAA) provided in the states we visited. Among these elder justice services were basic legal services to older adults, such as assisting with setting up wills, power of attorney, or advance directives, which can help deter financial exploitation. AAAs we visited also coordinated a number of other types of elder justice services. For example, an Arizona AAA administers a program funded through a Justice Victims of Crime Act grant to provide emergency housing for abused older adults. The same AAA uses HHS Title VII of the OAA funding for a Boys and Girls Club program to teach young people about respecting older adults. In Illinois, a Justice STOP grant helped create the Elder Law and Miscellaneous Remedies Division of the Circuit Court of Cook County which handles elder abuse cases and other instances where the victim is an older adult.

Officials representing all of the nine AAAs and nine of the local providers we interviewed also helped raise awareness of elder abuse through education and training programs both for the public in general and for those members of the community who regularly interact directly with older adults. For example, in Virginia, a local service provider received a Justice grant to train criminal justice professional service providers, victims, witnesses, and anyone likely to come in contact with elders. Such individuals may not be aware of the different ways abuse can present itself in the older adult population, and other AAA officials said that education and training for these direct service providers could help them identify it and respond appropriately. The Virginia provider saw its program as helpful in determining how to address an abused older adult's problems. In our view, in the absence of this awareness, incidents of elder abuse may go unreported or unaddressed.

For the most part, APS agencies in Arizona and Virginia worked with AAAs to identify and respond to incidents of elder abuse. Although the administrative structure of the AAAs and APS agencies can vary from state to state, the basic AAA services can help bolster an older adult's independence after an elder abuse incident. Depending on the division of responsibility for elder justice services in the state, AAAs may refer reports of elder abuse to the state's APS program in their area. For example, in Arizona and Virginia, the AAAs turn any allegations of elder abuse over to the state APS program upon learning about it. However, in Illinois, the state contracts with service providers to conduct the entire investigation and disposition of the elder abuse cases. Once an investigation has been conducted and service needs identified, AAAs may be involved in connecting elder abuse victims to services.

Despite their efforts to raise awareness of elder abuse in their communities, officials at five AAAs and four local service providers told us that more public awareness and training was needed. Moreover, officials from state aging agencies in two of the three states we visited said that the federal government should further emphasize the need for training law enforcement officers and other officials in identifying elder abuse for when they come in contact with older adults in need. An AAA official in one of these states said that training resources should also be directed to healthcare officials, because they are in a position to identify signs of elder abuse.

In prior work on elder financial exploitation, experts and federal, state, and local officials focusing on this form of elder abuse told us that older adults need more information about what constitutes financial exploitation to know how to avoid it. That prior study found that each of the seven federal agencies reviewed independently produces and disseminates public information on elder financial exploitation that is tailored to its own mission, and worked together at times to increase public awareness. For example, each year, the FTC and the Postal Inspection Service collaborate on community presentations during National Consumer Protection Week. However, although the Older Americans Act calls for a coordinated federal elder justice system, which includes educating the public, the seven agencies reviewed in that prior study did not undertake these activities as part of a broader coordinated approach.[37] In other work on public program effectiveness, we have concluded that agencies can use limited funding more efficiently by coordinating their activities and can strengthen their collaboration by establishing joint strategies.[38]

Of the nine AAA officials we spoke with for this review, five said that there is a need for a strategic, national public awareness campaign on elder justice, not limited to financial exploitation. Officials at three of these AAAs suggested that the federal government sponsor a national campaign to raise awareness that would include broadly dispersed public education announcements on the prevalence and types of elder abuse and helpful resources for those in need. The campaign would help service providers and care givers who interact with older adults or observe their behavior recognize the signs of elder abuse and report it.

[37] GAO, *Elder Justice: National Strategy Needed to Effectively Combat Financial Exploitation*, GAO-13-110 (Washington, D.C.: Nov. 15, 2012).

[38] GAO-06-15.

During its meeting in May 2013 to consider next steps, the Elder Justice Coordinating Council moved closer to developing a coordinated federal effort to prevent and respond to elder abuse. One of the actions recommended by the Council's Federal Interagency Working Group was the development of a national public awareness campaign. However, the Council is currently considering this recommendation and has not yet taken a final decision. Our work for this study indicates that until a broad-based public awareness campaign is established, many incidents of elder abuse may be unreported or unaddressed.

## Conclusions

Growth in the percentage of the United States population over 60 years of age and in reports of elder abuse may outstrip the public resources allocated to serve the elderly. In addition, given the range of elder justice activities and individuals served under federal programs, coordination is key to ensuring the efficient use of limited resources. Further, while federal agencies have taken some initial steps toward coordinating their elder justice activities, such as forming the Elder Justice Coordinating Council, their efforts to develop a coordinated response to elder abuse would be further supported by an assessment of the effectiveness of federal elder justice programs. Until common objectives and outcomes for federal elder justice programs are defined, agencies may be working at cross purposes. In addition, with the continuing growth in the older adult population, the absence of sufficient public awareness and education about elder abuse and the resources available to address it may slow the progress of elder justice efforts at all levels of government.

## Recommendations for Executive Action

1. To provide the basis for greater consistency across states in assessing elder justice service delivery, we recommend that the Secretary of HHS, as chairman of the Elder Justice Coordinating Council, direct the Council to make it a priority to identify common objectives for the federal elder justice effort and define common outcomes.

2. To help protect older adults from all forms of abuse, we recommend that the Secretary of HHS and the Attorney General collaborate in developing a national campaign to raise awareness of the occurrence of elder abuse and provide information on how to obtain services.

## Agency Comments and Our Evaluation

We provided a draft of this report to HHS and Justice, the two federal agencies that administer the 12 elder justice programs that we reviewed. HHS provided general comments that are reproduced in appendix III.

Both departments provided technical comments, which we incorporated as appropriate.

HHS concurred with our recommendations and agreed that federal coordination is key to ensuring the use of limited resources. Concerning the first recommendation, HHS identified the formation of the Elder Justice Coordinating Council as an effort to develop common objectives and plans for action to address elder justice issues. Further, HHS said that each of nine proposals for action that the Council now is considering has specified outcomes and that steps and strategies are being developed to implement the proposals. We agree that the Council's activity is indicative of progress toward a coordinated federal elder justice effort and development of common objectives. We encourage the Council to think broadly in developing common objectives and outcomes that will encompass the elder justice programs of all federal agencies represented on the Council, both now and in the future. HHS said that our recommendations correctly point out a need for greater public awareness and, with regard to the second recommendation, that one of the proposals for Council action is development of a broad-based public awareness campaign.

HHS also asked us to consider that improved public surveillance could help better describe the extent and patterns of abuse among older adults. In our previous report on elder abuse,[39] we noted that, although the CDC considers elder abuse a growing public health problem, there is no ongoing surveillance of its extent similar to periodic national incidence studies of child abuse and neglect. Without periodically measuring the extent of elder abuse nationwide, it will be difficult to develop an effective national policy for its prevention as required under the OAA.[40] In that report, we suggest that Congress consider mandating the Secretary of HHS to conduct, in coordination with the Attorney General, a periodic national study of the extent of elder abuse over time.

---

[39]GAO-11-208

[40] 42 U.S.C. § 3011(e)(2).

We are sending copies of this report to the appropriate congressional committees, the Secretaries of the Departments of Health and Human Services and Justice, and other interested parties. We will also make copies available to others on request. In addition, the report will be available at no charge on GAO's website at http://www.gao.gov. If you or your staff have any questions about this report, please contact me at (202) 512-7215 or brownke@gao.gov. Contact points for our Office of Congressional Relations and Public Affairs can be found on the last page of this report. GAO staff who made major contributions to this report are listed in appendix VI.

Kay E. Brown
Director
Education, Workforce, and Income Security Issues

# Appendix I: Scope and Methodology for Surveying Federal Elder Justice Program Managers

This appendix discusses the methodology for surveying federal elder justice program managers to gather information for examining the potential for fragmentation, overlap, and duplication among federal elder justice programs.

Using lists of existing federal programs, we identified programs government-wide that funded elder justice activities, based on program selection criteria discussed below. We confirmed the list through contact with federal agency officials. We surveyed the federal officials who manage the federal elder justice programs on our list, and analyzed the programs' similarities and differences with regard to key elements, including objectives, activities, funding mechanisms and recipients, target populations, outcome measures and fiscal year 2011 obligations.

## Identification of Federal Elder Justice Programs

For the purposes of this study, we defined elder justice as efforts to prevent, identify, and respond to elder abuse. To identify federal programs that provided funding for elder justice activities in fiscal year 2011, we developed an initial list of programs that met our definition of elder justice and one of three selection criteria, as shown in figure 4.

**Figure 4: Elder Justice Program Selection Criteria**

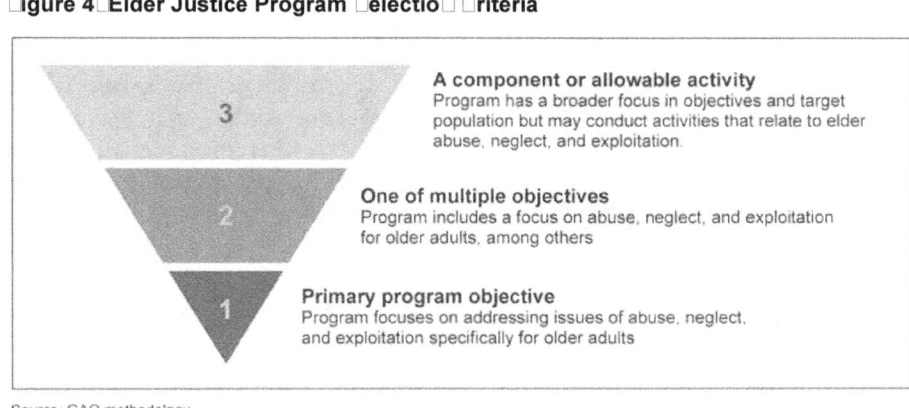

**3** — **A component or allowable activity**
Program has a broader focus in objectives and target population but may conduct activities that relate to elder abuse, neglect, and exploitation.

**2** — **One of multiple objectives**
Program includes a focus on abuse, neglect, and exploitation for older adults, among others

**1** — **Primary program objective**
Program focuses on addressing issues of abuse, neglect, and exploitation specifically for older adults

Source: GAO methodology.

The list was based on the findings of three prior inventory efforts completed by GAO and the Congressional Research Service in 2011, as well as searches of the Catalog of Federal Domestic Assistance and agency websites. To confirm the programs on our list, we contacted agency officials who managed the programs during our entrance conferences for additional program information. We also asked agency officials to add any programs that we had overlooked in developing the list. We then reassessed the list to determine how well the programs met the elder justice definition and program selection criteria.

## Survey of Federal Elder Justice Program Managers

To determine how federal programs that target elder justice compare with respect to key elements, we developed a web-based survey to collect descriptive information about programs from agency officials. Because program obligations during fiscal year 2011 was one of the data elements we needed to collect, the survey was designed to collect information from programs that either have elder justice as a primary objective or one of multiple objectives.

To develop the survey questions, we reviewed prior GAO reports on elder justice, on serving the aging population, and on identifying duplication and overlap in federal programs administered by multiple agencies. The survey, modeled after GAO surveys regarding potential overlap and duplication, collected information on key program elements pertaining to overlap and duplication, including objectives, activities, target populations, outcome measures, and obligations during fiscal year 2011. The survey was administered between July and September 2012. To maximize response, we sent periodic follow-up emails to all agency officials that had not responded to the survey by our deadline.

The practical difficulties of conducting any survey may introduce several types of errors, commonly referred to as non-sampling errors. For example, differences in how a particular question is interpreted, the sources of information available to respondents, or the types of people who do not respond can introduce unwanted variability into the survey results. We included steps in the survey design, data collection, and data analysis to minimize such non-sampling errors. In designing the survey, we took steps to clarify the survey questions to ensure that questions would be correctly interpreted by respondents. For example, during its development, we pretested our Web-based survey with five selected programs administered by HHS, Justice, and the SEC. We conducted these pretests to ensure that the respondents understood the questions and could provide the answers to them and the questions could be completed in a reasonable amount of time. Following each pretest, the survey underwent additional, mostly minor, revisions, based on feedback from pretest participants. An additional source of non-sampling error can be errors in computer processing of the data and statistical analysis. All computer programs relied on for analysis of this survey data were independently verified by a second analyst for accuracy.

The survey response rate was 100 percent. In addition to collecting program information, the survey allowed us to confirm, exclude, and add programs based on consultations with agency officials. As a result of our analysis of the survey data, including follow-up contact with the agency officials who managed them, we identified 12 programs that met one of the first two selection criteria and funded elder justice activities in fiscal year 2011. We analyzed whether similarities and differences in the 12 programs with respect to key program elements, such as sponsoring agency, objectives, activities, target populations and grant recipients, indicated potential overlap or duplication, and whether program officials could identify program outcomes.

To augment the survey data, we collected additional information on program activities and target groups for individual activities. We reviewed program descriptions published on agency websites, in grant solicitations, and in budget justifications; and reviewed publicly available lists of grant recipients and award amounts. We then grouped activity descriptions by type of activity and specific group or subpopulation that directly benefited from the activity. For example, we determined whether education and outreach efforts were directed at the general public or a specific subpopulation of victims of elder abuse, such as those in tribal communities. We confirmed these classifications with the relevant program officials and added or corrected information as necessary.

# Appendix II: Federal Elder Justice Programs

**Table 3: Federal Programs That Directed All Funds toward Elder Justice Ranked by Fiscal Year 2011 obligations**

| Department/agency | Program | Objectives and examples of elder justice activities | Fiscal Year 2011 obligations |
|---|---|---|---|
| Justice/OVW | Enhanced Training and Services to End Violence Against and Abuse of Women Later in Life Program | **Objectives:** <br><br>• Enhance the ability of criminal justice professionals, government agency staff, and victim assistants to address elder abuse, neglect, and exploitation, including domestic violence, dating violence, sexual assault, and stalking, in their communities. <br><br>• Develop or enhance a coordinated community response to elder abuse. <br><br>• Provide or enhance services for victims who are 50 years of age or older. <br><br>• Conduct cross-training for victim service organizations, governmental agencies; criminal justice professionals; and nonprofit, nongovernmental organizations serving victims of elder abuse, neglect, and exploitation, including sexual assault, domestic violence, dating violence, and stalking, in their communities. <br><br>**Examples of elder justice activities:** <br><br>• Develop multidisciplinary partnerships that include law enforcement, prosecutors, domestic violence victim services programs or nonprofits, and programs or nonprofits that serve older victims. <br><br>• Training for law enforcement officers, prosecutors, judges, and individuals that serve older victims and work in victims services programs. <br><br>• Cross training for victim services organizations, governmental agencies, courts, law enforcement agencies, and organizations working with older victims. <br><br>• Outreach and service delivery to older victims. | $5,249,000[a] |

| Department/ agency | Program | Objectives and examples of elder justice activities | Fiscal Year 2011 obligations |
|---|---|---|---|
| HHS/ACL | Prevention of Elder Abuse, Neglect, and Exploitation | **Objective:** <br><br>• Support activities to develop, strengthen, and carry out programs for the prevention, detection, assessment, and treatment of, intervention in, investigation of, and response to elder abuse, neglect, and exploitation, including financial exploitation.[b] <br><br>**Examples of elder justice activities:** <br><br>• Training law enforcement officers, health care providers, and other professionals on how to recognize and respond to elder abuse. <br><br>• Support outreach and education campaigns to increase public awareness of elder abuse and prevention, including financial exploitation. <br><br>• Support efforts of state and local elder abuse prevention coalitions and multidisciplinary teams of agencies and organizations that work with victims. <br><br>• Promote the development of information and data systems, including elder abuse reporting systems, to quantify the extent of elder abuse in each state and analyze information to identify unmet service and need. <br><br>• Provide technical assistance to programs that provide services for victims of elder abuse and their families. | $5,033,000 |
| Justice/OJP | Coordinated Tribal Assistance Solicitations: Tribal Elder Outreach Program | **Objectives:** <br><br>• Develop comprehensive outreach strategies and foster improved culturally appropriate crime victim assistance services to address elder abuse. <br><br>• Augment ongoing crime victim assistance service strategies and provide special focus on elders including enhanced collaboration and coordination among victim assistance and human services, courts and law enforcement, and community development and youth outreach and mentoring programs. <br><br>• Link the issue of elder abuse in tribal communities with traditional cultural norms of respect and reverence for tribal elders. <br><br>**Examples of elder justice activities:** <br><br>• Conduct outreach through awareness posters, service brochures, editorials and newspaper articles, radio and television ads, videos, and fact sheets. <br><br>• Support curriculum development, training, community teaching, and awareness efforts. <br><br>• Promote community-based and culturally specific crime victim assistance services and develop and distribute related protocols and toolkits. | $1,454,000 |

| Department/ agency | Program | Objectives and examples of elder justice activities | Fiscal Year 2011 obligations |
|---|---|---|---|
| HHS/NIH | National Institute on Aging (NIA) Research Activities Related to Elder Mistreatment | **Objective**<br>• Support research on elder mistreatment and related issues.<br>**Examples of elder justice activities**<br>• Conduct targeted research related to elder mistreatment. Specific projects include:<br> ○ Epidemiological study of the relationship of self-neglect and important health outcomes in a biracial population of older adults.<br> ○ Study of relevant health issues, including elder mistreatment, in older Chinese adults.<br> ○ Development of a mentoring program for aspiring researchers on aging topics.<br> ○ Study to determine the extent and outcomes of resident-to-resident elder mistreatment in long-term care facilities.<br> ○ Studies of the social and neural bases for older adults' vulnerability to financial exploitation. | $1,134,000 |
| HHS/ACL | National Center on Elder Abuse | **Objective**<br>• Provide information, materials, and support to enhance state and local efforts to prevent and address elder mistreatment.<br>**Examples of elder justice activities**<br>• Disseminate information about elder abuse prevention, including promising practices and interventions, and provide resources to professionals and the public.<br>• Provide technical assistance, training, and consultation, to state agencies and community-based organizations.<br>• Advise on program and policy development. | $804,000 |
| Justice/Civil Division | Elder Justice and Nursing Home Initiative | **Objective**<br>• Support and coordinate Justice's activities in combating elder abuse, neglect, and financial exploitation, especially as they impact beneficiaries of Medicare, Medicaid, and other federal health care programs.<br>**Examples of elder justice activities**<br>• Prosecute failure of care, health care fraud, and consumer fraud cases and enforce civil rights.<br>• Promote state and local coordination through state working groups.<br>• Provide training for U.S. Attorney's offices and Medicaid Fraud Control Units on investigating and developing failure of care cases.<br>• Provide training for nurses, prosecutors, judges, and participants of legal aid clinics on fraud and abuse cases. | $747,000[a] |

| Department/ agency | Program | Objectives and examples of elder justice activities | Fiscal Year 2011 obligations |
|---|---|---|---|
| HHS/ACL | National Adult Protective Services (APS) Resource Center | **Objective**<br><br>• Enhance the quality, consistency, and effectiveness of APS programs across the country, with a primary focus on the older population, by providing APS systems, agencies, and professionals with relevant information and support.<br><br>**Examples of elder justice activities**<br><br>• Identify evidence-based practices for APS programs and interventions and promote the evaluation of unevaluated practices that have the potential to advance and strengthen the efficiency, effectiveness, and relevance of APS work.<br><br>• Compile and synthesize research that informs APS programming and interventions.<br><br>• Provide specific and targeted technical assistance to state and local APS programs to facilitate the implementation of best practices and research findings. | 200,000 |

Source: GAO analysis of GAO survey data.

[a]Reported by agency officials.

[b]ACL is broadly responsible for federal efforts related to elder abuse and prevention services. In addition to administering individual programs, ACL is responsible for facilitating the development, implementation, and improvement of a coordinated, multidisciplinary elder justice system; providing federal leadership to support state efforts to carry out elder justice programs; establishing an information clearinghouse; and promoting collaborative efforts for the development and implementation of elder justice programs. 42 U.S.C. § 3011(a).

**Table 5: Federal Programs that Directed Some Funds toward Elder Justice (ranked by FY2011 obligations)**

| Department/ agency | Program | Objectives and examples of elder justice activities | Fiscal Year 2011 obligations[a] |
|---|---|---|---|
| Justice/OVW | Services, Training, Officers, and Prosecutors (STOP) Violence Against Women Formula Grant Program | **Objectives:**<br><br>• Support communities in their efforts to develop and strengthen effective law enforcement and prosecution strategies to combat violent crimes against women, including older women.<br><br>• Develop and strengthen victim services in cases involving violent crimes against women, including older women.<br><br>**Examples of elder justice activities:**<br><br>• Provide training for law enforcement officers, judges, other court personnel, prosecutors, and domestic violence victim service providers to more effectively identify and respond to violent crimes against women.<br><br>• Develop and implement more effective police, court, and prosecution policies and protocols regarding violent crimes against women.<br><br>• Develop data collection and communication systems linking police, prosecutors, and courts to identify and track arrests and violations.<br><br>• Support statewide multidisciplinary efforts to coordinate the response of state law enforcement agencies, prosecutors, courts, victim services agencies, and other state agencies.<br><br>• Provide training for sexual assault forensic medical examiners in collecting evidence.<br><br>• Strengthen programs that address violence against older women and women with disabilities, including investigating and prosecuting instances of violence and targeting outreach, counseling, and other victim assistance services. | $136,620,000[b] |

| Department/agency | Program | Objectives and examples of elder justice activities | Fiscal Year 2011 obligations |
|---|---|---|---|
| Justice/OVW | Grants to Encourage Arrest Policies and Enforcement of Protection Orders Program | **Objectives**<br><br>• Encourage state, local, and tribal governments and courts to treat domestic violence, dating violence, sexual assault, and stalking, including instances of violence against older individuals, as serious violations of criminal law.<br><br>**Examples of elder justice activities**<br><br>• Implement pro-arrest programs and policies, including programs that train police, prosecutors, and the judiciary in addressing instances of abuse.<br><br>• Educate judges in criminal and civil courts about assault, domestic violence, dating violence, and stalking.<br><br>• Coordinate computer tracking systems to ensure communication between police, prosecutors, parole and probation officers, and criminal and family courts.<br><br>• Develop protection order registries and provide technical assistance and equipment to law enforcement and legal departments to facilitate enforcement of protection orders.<br><br>• Develop methods for identifying the pattern and history of abuse.<br><br>• Establish comprehensive victim service and support centers to improve safety, access to services, and confidentiality for victims and families. | $44,602,000[a] |
| HHS/CDC | Interpersonal Violence within Families and Among Acquaintances Prevention | **Objective**<br><br>• Prevent interpersonal violence – including domestic violence, sexual assault, spousal and partner abuse, and elder abuse, woman battering, and acquaintance rape – within families and among acquaintances.<br><br>**Examples of elder justice activities**<br><br>• Develop uniform definitions and recommend data elements for public health surveillance of elder abuse and neglect.<br><br>• Provide information and education to the public on interpersonal violence to increase awareness of related public health consequences.<br><br>• Provide training to health care providers to identify potential victims of interpersonal violence and refer individuals to entities that provide supportive services. | $26,634,000[b,c] |
| HHS/ACL | Long-Term Care (LTC) Ombudsman Program | **Objectives**<br><br>• Advocate for residents of nursing homes, board and care homes, assisted living facilities, and similar adult care facilities and improve residents' care and quality of life.<br><br>• Resolve problems of individual residents.<br><br>**Examples of elder justice activities**<br><br>• Investigate and resolve complaints made by residents of facilities.<br><br>• Provide training to state and local ombudsmen.<br><br>• Provide consultations to LTC facility managers and staff. | $16,749,000 |

| Department/agency[c] | Program | Objectives and examples of elder justice activities | Fiscal Year 2011 obligations[b] |
|---|---|---|---|
| HHS/ACL | National Long-Term Care Ombudsman Resource Center | **Objectives:**<br>• Enhance the skills, knowledge, and management capacity of state LTC ombudsman programs to enable them to effectively respond to residents' complaints and represent their interests on an individual and systemic level.<br>• Strengthen the LTC Ombudsman program by developing innovative, effective approaches for states to provide services to LTC facility residents.<br>**Examples of elder justice activities:**<br>• Provide technical assistance to state and local ombudsmen.<br>• Provide consultation, information, and referral for ombudsmen, residents, and families.<br>• Provide training and resources for state and local ombudsman programs.<br>• Promote public awareness on the role of ombudsmen.<br>• Identify research needs and promote research related to ombudsman programs and services.<br>• Promote cooperation between ombudsman programs and advocacy groups. | $574,000 |

Source: GAO analysis of GAO survey data.

[a]Amounts reflect spending on all program activities, including those unrelated to elder justice, as obligations are not tracked separately by activity, according to officials.

[b]Reported by agency officials.

[c]The CDC later reported that this amount reflects spending on all program activities, including those unrelated to elder justice, as obligations are not tracked separately by activity. However, program officials estimated that the amount spent on elder justice activities in fiscal year 2011 was $50,000.

Table 8: Federal Programs with Elder Justice as a Program Component or Allowable Activity Listed by Agency in Alphabetical Order[a]

| Department/agency | Program | Objectives[b] | Examples of activities related to elder justice |
|---|---|---|---|
| Federal Trade Commission (FTC)/Bureau of Consumer Protection | Consumer Education | Educate consumers and businesses about their rights and responsibilities, including providing consumers with tools needed to make informed decisions and businesses with tools needed to comply with law. | Provides free information to consumers of all ages. The FTC identifies older adults as a target population for many of its consumer education efforts, including how to recognize and report identity theft and scams/frauds related to health care and financial exploitation. |
| FTC/Bureau of Consumer Protection | Consumer Protection Law Enforcement | Enforce consumer protection laws in federal court or administrative litigation, especially in cases alleging deceptive practices; coordinate joint law enforcement actions with state and federal partners, including criminal law enforcement; enforce injunctions and administrative orders obtained in consumer protection cases; and develop, review, and enforce consumer protection rules. | The Bureau of Consumer Protection has investigated frauds affecting seniors, and misrepresentations aimed at the "oldest old" and their caretakers, including misrepresentations of services provided when referring seniors to long-term care facilities. |
| FTC/Bureau of Consumer Protection | Consumer Sentinel Network | Collect consumer complaint data and share information to enable state and local law enforcement to become more effective. | Collects and stores information on consumer complaints, including financial exploitation incidents such as investment fraud and identify theft. Complaints may include those reported by older individuals, though the FTC does not require complaints to include the age of the victim. |
| HHS/Administration for Children and Families (ACF) | Community Services Block Grant | Provide assistance to states, U.S. territories, and tribal governments, to provide services and activities to reduce poverty. | Grants support activities that address nutrition, health, and emergency services, among others, for low-income individuals including the elderly. |
| HHS/ACF | Social Services Block Grant | Reduce or eliminate dependency; achieve or maintain self-sufficiency for families; help prevent neglect, abuse, or exploitation of children and adults; prevent or reduce inappropriate institutional care; and secure admission or referral for institutional care when other forms of care are not appropriate. | Grants may be used to support activities aimed at preventing neglect, abuse, or exploitation of children or adults, among others. |

| Department/agency | Program | Objectives | Examples of activities related to elder justice |
|---|---|---|---|
| HHS/ACL | Home and Community-Based Supportive Services [Supportive Services and Senior Centers Program] | Provide formula grants to states to support services that enable seniors to remain in their homes for as long as possible. | Services may include case management and legal services, among others. Each state may allocate funds to area agencies on aging, which have the flexibility to use the funds to provide the services that best meet the needs of seniors in their service areas. In providing community services, providers could observe and report on potential elder abuse activity. |
| HHS/ACL | Legal Assistance Developer | Promote and enhance state leadership in securing and maintaining legal rights of older individuals and state capacity to: coordinate the provision of legal assistance, provide technical assistance and training; promote financial management services for older individuals, assist older individuals in understanding their rights, and improve the quality and quantity of legal services provided to older adults. | The legal assistance developer can play a key role in designing and implementing the elder rights provisions of state plans to ensure older persons have access to their benefits and rights. |
| HHS/ACL | Legal Assistance–Title III-B Providers | Provide assistance for older individuals in accessing long-term care options and other community-based services; protect older individuals against direct challenges to their independence, choice, and financial security. | Services are specifically targeted to older individuals with economic or social needs. Services may include assistance to ensure elder rights protections regarding transfers from LTC facilities to home and community-based care and assistance for individuals who have experienced elder abuse, including consumer fraud and financial exploitation. |
| HHS/ACL | Model Approaches to Statewide Legal Assistance Systems | Provide funding to strengthen states' legal services networks, including the development and implementation of integrating low-cost service mechanisms. | Grants support legal education and assistance services and may include projects that address elder financial exploitation. The program also promotes linkages with service providers in area aging agencies, Aging and Disability Resource Centers, state long-term care ombudsmen, and APS. |
| HHS/ACL | National Family Caregiver Support Program | Provide grants to states to assist family and informal caregivers to care for loved ones at home for as long as possible. | Services include dissemination of information about services and other assistance including counseling and training. |

| Department/ agency | Program | Objective(s) | Examples of activities related to elder justice |
|---|---|---|---|
| HHS/ACL | National Legal Resource Center | Support the aging and legal networks to enhance the quality, cost effectiveness, and accessibility of legal assistance and elder rights programs; and support demonstration projects to expand or improve the delivery of legal assistance and elder rights protections to older individuals with social or economic needs. | Supported activities include case consultation for legal professionals regarding legal problems impacting older individuals, training for aging and legal services professionals on a range of legal and elder rights issues, technical assistance to professionals that provide legal assistance to older individuals, and information dissemination regarding legal and elder rights issues. |
| HHS/ACL | Nutrition Services (Congregate Nutrition Services, Home-Delivered Nutrition Services and Nutrition Services Incentive Program) | Reduce hunger and food insecurity, promote socialization of older individuals, and promote the health and well-being of older individuals and delay health conditions through access to nutrition and other disease prevention and health promotion services. | Grants to states support nutrition services including meals and nutrition education. In providing or delivering meals, service providers could observe and report on potential elder abuse activity. |
| HHS/ACL | Pension Counseling and Information Program | Promote the financial security of older individuals and enhance their choice and independence by empowering them to make decisions with respect to pensions and savings plans. | Projects include assisting seniors with the administrative appeals process, locating pension plans "lost" as a result of mergers and acquisitions, and other assistance in negotiating with former employers for due compensation. |
| HHS/ACL | Resource Centers for Older Indians, Alaskan Natives, and Native Hawaiians | Provide culturally competent health care, community-based long-term care, and related services; serve as focal points for developing and sharing technical information and expertise for organizations, communities, educational institutions, and professionals working with older Native Americans. | Center activities have included assisting in developing community-based solutions to improve the quality of life and delivery of support services to the Native elderly population and providing a forum for discussions about elder abuse to help communities develop plans to reduce and control occurrences. |
| HHS/ACL | Senior Medicare Patrol | Empower seniors to protect themselves from the economic and health-related consequences of Medicare and Medicaid fraud, error, and abuse through increased awareness and understanding of health care programs. | Activities include training Medicare beneficiaries, retired professionals, and other senior citizens on how to recognize and report instances or patterns of health care fraud and abuse and complaint resolution for beneficiaries. |
| HHS/Centers for Medicare and Medicaid Services (CMS) | Nationwide Program for National and State Background Checks for Direct Patient Access Employees of Long-Term Care (LTC) Facilities and Providers | Identify efficient, effective, and economical procedures for LTC facilities and providers to conduct background checks on a statewide basis on all prospective direct patient access employees. | States conduct background checks to help meet regulations prohibiting LTC facilities and providers from employing individuals found guilty of abuse, neglect, or misappropriation of patient funds. |

| Department/ agency | Program | Objectives | Examples of activities related to elder justice |
|---|---|---|---|
| HHS/CMS | Office of the Medicare Ombudsman Response to Inquiries and Complaints | Receive complaints, grievances, and requests for information from, and provide assistance to, Medicare beneficiaries. | The ombudsman may receive inquiries or complaints that mention elder abuse and refer complainants to the appropriate agency or organization to address their concerns. |
| HHS/CMS | Survey and Certification of Medicaid and Medicare Providers and Suppliers | Determine whether service providers and suppliers meet applicable requirements for participation in Medicare and/or Medicaid programs, and are incompliance with Medicaid and Medicare conditions of participation and coverage. | Federal and state surveyors conduct health and safety inspections in a variety of settings, including nursing homes, home health agencies, and hospitals, to determine compliance with CMS regulations including those that address abuse and neglect of beneficiaries. |
| HHS/Health Resources and Services Administration (HRSA) | Comprehensive Geriatric Education Program | Train and educate individuals in providing geriatric care for the elderly. | Activities include training, development of curricula related to the treatment of health problems of the elderly, continuing education, and establishment of traineeships for advanced education students. |
| HHS/HRSA | Geriatric Academic Career Awards [b] | Support the career development of physicians, nurses, social workers, psychologists, dentists, pharmacists, and health professionals as academic geriatric specialist by requiring them to provide training in clinical geriatrics, including the training of interdisciplinary teams of health professionals. | Faculty teaches and develops skills in interdisciplinary education geriatrics. |
| HHS/HRSA | Geriatric Education Centers [b] | Establish or operate Geriatric Education Centers to provide interdisciplinary training of health professional faculty, students, and practitioners in the diagnosis, treatment and prevention of disease, disability, and other health problems of the elderly. | Project activities include training and continuing education of health professionals in geriatrics and developing curricula related to the treatment of health problems of the elderly. |
| HHS/HRSA | Geriatric Training for Physicians, Dentists and Behavioral/Mental Health Professionals [b] | Provide support, including fellowships, for geriatric training projects to train physicians, dentists and behavioral or mental health professionals who plan to teach geriatric medicine, geriatric dentistry, or geriatric behavioral or mental health. | Physicians participate in service rotations that include day and home care programs, extended care facilities, and community care programs. |
| Department of Housing and Urban Development (HUD)/Office of Housing | Home Equity Conversion Mortgage Program | Provide eligible homeowners with education and information about the unique features of a reverse mortgage and other alternatives to a reverse mortgage that homeowners may consider given their financial situation. | HUD offers counseling to elderly clients who may be at risk of delinquency in paying mortgages and may be at risk of becoming victims of financial exploitation. |

| Department/ agency | Program | Objectives | Examples of activities related to elder justice |
|---|---|---|---|
| HUD/Office of Housing | Multifamily Housing Service Coordinators | Extend the length and improve the quality of independent living and prevent premature and inappropriate institutionalization of elderly and disabled non-elderly residents of federally-assisted multifamily housing. | Service coordinators assess resident needs; identify and link residents to appropriate services in the community, and monitor the delivery of services. Service coordinators may also educate residents about other services and help them build informal support networks. |
| HUD/Office of Public and Indian Housing | Resident Opportunities and Self-Sufficiency | Link public housing residents with supportive services, resident empowerment activities, and assistance in becoming economically self-sufficient. For elderly or disabled residents specifically, the objective is to help improve living conditions and enable residents to age-in-place. | Service coordinators assess the needs of residents and coordinate available resources, including supportive services for elderly residents. |
| Justice/Office of Community Oriented Policing Services | Coordinated Tribal Assistance Solicitations: Tribal Resources Grant Program | Address the most serious tribal law enforcement needs; increase the capacity of tribal law enforcement agencies to prevent, solve, and control crime for safer communities; implement or enhance community policing strategies; and engage in strategic planning for law enforcement. | Grants support law enforcement training, including community policing and computer and crime reporting training. |
| Justice/National Institutes of Justice | National Institutes of Justice Research, Evaluation, and Development Project Grants | Encourage and support research, development, and evaluation to further understanding of the causes and correlates of crime and violence, methods of crime prevention and control, and criminal justice system responses to crime and violence; and contribute to the improvement of the criminal justice system and its responses to crime, violence, and delinquency. | Projects include research related to elder mistreatment as it relates to the objectives of the program, such as identifying the causes and means of preventing crime. |
| Justice/OVW | Coordinated Tribal Assistance Solicitations: Grants to Indian Tribal Governments Program | Enhance the systemic response to crimes of domestic violence, dating violence, sexual assault, and stalking committed against American Indian and Alaska Native women and girls. | Victim services provided under the program, including emergency shelter services, crisis intervention, and information and referrals, may be provided to older individuals who are victims. |
| Securities and Exchange Commission (SEC)/Division of Enforcement | Enforcement Actions in General Prosecuted by the Division of Enforcement | Provide investor protection through the prosecution of violations of federal of securities laws. | Prosecuted cases may include those involving older adults as victims. In some instances, the elderly were specifically targeted. |
| SEC/Division of Enforcement | Outreach Activities to Prevent Financial Exploitation of Investors | Provide information to investors about protecting their finances, funds and investments, and ways regulators can support their efforts. | While most outreach activities are targeted at all investors, there are several activities, throughout the country, that are specifically focused on senior investors, such as Senior Summits, Senior Days and Senior Expos. |

| Department/ agency[a] | Program | Objectives[b] | Examples of activities related to elder justice |
|---|---|---|---|
| SEC/Division of Trading and Markets | Division of Trading and Markets Outreach Activities | Engage in outreach activities on an ad hoc basis. | Past activities have included SEC's Senior Summits which help older investors make difficult decisions about their finances and learn new ways to protect their assets as they age. |
| SEC/Office of Compliance Inspections and Examinations | Examinations in General Conducted by the Office of Compliance Inspections and Examinations | Foster compliance with securities laws, detect violations, and correct compliance problems by conducting examinations of registered entities, broker-dealers, and investment advisers and companies, among others. | Examinations may identify unsuitable transactions for senior investors. |
| SEC/Office of Investor Education and Advocacy (OIEA) | Outreach Activities to Inform Investors | Provide investors with information needed to evaluate current and potential investments, make informed decisions, and avoid fraudulent schemes. In addition, provide agency staff with critical insight about emerging trends and factors shaping investor decision-making. | OIEA may target certain outreach efforts to specific groups, such as seniors, members of the military, and teachers. Outreach includes providing resources to help individuals become better-educated investors, including understanding how to avoid fraud. For example, OIEA continues to support the Outsmarting Investment Fraud Campaign, designed to educate seniors about identifying potential investment fraud. |
| Department of the Treasury/Financial Crimes Enforcement Network (FinCEN) | FinCEN Advisories and Public Education/ Outreach Efforts | Communicate money laundering or terrorist financing risks to the financial industry and facilitate the reporting of valuable information to law enforcement. | FinCEN issued an advisory to financial institutions in 2011 that provided potential indicators of elder financial exploitation. |

Source: GAO analysis of agency documentation.

[a]We surveyed programs with elder justice as a primary objective or one of multiple objectives. Programs with elder justice as a program component or allowable activity were not within the scope of our survey and therefore we did not collect obligations data for these programs or verify that obligations were made to these programs in fiscal year 2011. We also did not independently verify the agency documentation gathered from program officials or agency web sites.

[b]HHS also refers collectively to these programs—Geriatric Academic Career Awards, Geriatric Education Centers, and Geriatric Training for Physicians, Dentists and Behavioral/Mental Health Professionals—as the Education and Training Relating to Geriatrics program

# Appendix III: Comments from the U.S. Department of Health and Human Services

DEPARTMENT OF HEALTH & HUMAN SERVICES     OFFICE OF THE SECRETARY

Assistant Secretary for Legislation
Washington, DC 20201

Kay E. Brown, Director
Education, Workforce, and Income Security Issues
U.S. Government Accountability Office
441 G Street NW
Washington, DC 20548

Dear Ms. Brown:

Attached are comments on the U.S. Government Accountability Office's (GAO) report entitled,
"Elder Justice: More Federal Coordination and Public Awareness Needed" (GAO-13-498).

The Department appreciates the opportunity to review this report prior to publication.

Sincerely,

Jim R. Esquea
Assistant Secretary for Legislation

Attachment

**GENERAL COMMENTS OF THE DEPARTMENT OF HEALTH AND HUMAN SERVICES (HHS) ON THE GOVERNMENT ACCOUNTABILITY OFFICE'S (GAO) DRAFT REPORT ENTITLED, "ELDER JUSTICE: MORE FEDERAL COORDINATION AND PUBLIC AWARENESS NEEDED" (GAO-13-498)**

The Department appreciates the opportunity to review and comment on this draft report.

The report notes the limited, non-duplicative nature of federal programs designed to address the numerous challenges associated with identifying, preventing and responding to elder abuse, neglect and exploitation at a time when older adults comprise an increasing proportion of the nation's population. To address this complicated problem, the Elder Justice Act (EJA) of 2009 provides the authority for a variety of initiatives needed to better address elder abuse. However, funding has not been appropriated to date to implement most of the activities contained in the EJA.

Consistent with this report's recommendation that federal coordination is key to ensuring the use of limited resources, the Elder Justice Coordinating Council (EJCC) has been convened in order to gather together relevant policymakers at the federal level to discuss how to develop common objectives and action plans. The EJCC held its inaugural meeting in October, 2012, at which time experts provided testimony and white papers with recommendations regarding elder justice activities and issues. The Elder Justice Working Group (EJWG), comprised of staff from the various agencies represented on the EJCC, reviewed this input and distilled the recommendations to nine proposals. The proposals were presented to the EJCC for consideration and input during a May, 2013 meeting. Each of the proposals represents a multi-agency, coordinated effort to provide federal leadership in addressing the major problems, issues, and gaps presented to the EJCC. Work is now underway to develop action steps and strategies for implementing these nine proposals, each of which have identified outcomes. These action steps will form the basis for a coordinated federal agenda, to be presented for consideration to the EJCC this fall. Among the nine proposals is one directed at developing and implementing a broad-based national public awareness campaign, as recommended in this report.

The proposals include:

1. Develop a national APS system based upon standardized data collection and a core set of service provision standards and best practices.

2. Establish a coordinated research agenda across federal agencies to identify best practices for prevention of and intervention in elder abuse and elder financial exploitation.

3. Enhance the ability of frontline professionals and first responders to identify diminished capacity broadly, to identify diminished financial capacity specifically, and to assess whether an older adult has been victimized or is particularly vulnerable to mistreatment.

4. Prevent, detect and redress elder financial exploitation by fiduciaries through improved coordination, oversight and education.

5. Bolster the ability of financial services providers to prevent, detect and respond to elder financial exploitation through guidance to industry from government, collaborative efforts, data-sharing, research and other strategies.

1

**GENERAL COMMENTS OF THE DEPARTMENT OF HEALTH AND HUMAN SERVICES (HHS) ON THE GOVERNMENT ACCOUNTABILITY OFFICE'S (GAO) DRAFT REPORT ENTITLED, "ELDER JUSTICE: MORE FEDERAL COORDINATION AND PUBLIC AWARENESS NEEDED" (GAO-13-498)**

6. Develop and implement a broad-based public awareness campaign.

7. Support the investigation and prosecution of elder abuse, neglect, and financial exploitation cases through the creation of a National Resource Center for the Investigation and Prosecution of Elder Abuse, an Elder Abuse Prosecution Website, and through the creation of a successful practices template for the development of additional Elder Abuse Forensic Centers.

8. Support and protect elder victims by enhancing identification of and response to elder abuse in all its forms.

9. Develop training to educate stakeholders across multiple sectors and disciplines on preventing, detecting, intervening in, and responding to elder abuse, neglect and exploitation.

Additionally, the National Institute on Aging sponsored a meeting of leading experts on elder mistreatment (EM) held at the National Academy of Sciences on June 22, 2010. The meeting was called to summarize the state-of-the-science in EM, identify gaps in knowledge, and elaborate upon the types of work needed to advance the science since the National Research Council's 2003 landmark publication *Elder Mistreatment: Abuse Neglect and Exploitation in an Aging America*. While NIA's primary interest is to advance research in the field, presenters' remarks were wide-ranging including comments on infrastructure development, funding, and criminal justice issues. Four categories of salient outcomes were noted (*emphasis added to those of most relevance to NIA*): (1) There is a need for interventions at all levels of the EM field including prevention, keeping abused elders in their own homes, clinical interventions, and legal/criminal justice interventions. (2) Measurement issues in EM have developed significantly, based upon NIA's funding of methodology development grants, and the field is ready to advance to a national prevalence/incidence study under the direction of agencies whose mission is closely aligned with prevalence/incidence detection such as CDC or DoJ. *(3) Financial fraud was identified as a significant problem with too little research being conducted on determining detection and prevention strategies.* (4) Finally, more general issues such *as research involving EM in minority populations,* career development of researchers in the field, and funding issues related to EM were discussed and identified as warranting greater attention and investment.

In response to those identified needs that fall within the NIA mission (Recommendations 3 and 4), the NIA will consider the following:
- Propose to continue to develop NIA research portfolio on financial decision making and susceptibility to fraud in older adults, closely linked to NIA existing research agenda in understanding the psychological and social determinants of healthy aging.
- Explore the extent to which minority populations are differentially or uniquely affected by this kind of elder abuse, and what research is needed to examine this issue.

2

GENERAL COMMENTS OF THE DEPARTMENT OF HEALTH AND HUMAN SERVICES (HHS) ON THE GOVERNMENT ACCOUNTABILITY OFFICE'S (GAO) DRAFT REPORT ENTITLED, "ELDER JUSTICE: MORE FEDERAL COORDINATION AND PUBLIC AWARENESS NEEDED" (GAO-13-498)

Lastly, the recommendations correctly point out a need for greater public awareness. Please consider that improved public health surveillance could help better describe the true extent and patterns of abuse and neglect among older adults.

3

# Appendix IV: GAO Contact and Staff Acknowledgments

| | |
|---|---|
| **GAO Contact** | Kay Brown, (202) 512-7215 or brownke@gao.gov |
| **Staff Acknowledgments:** | In addition to the contact listed above, individuals making key contributions to this report, in all aspects of the work, were Bill Keller, Sara Edmondson, Brenna Guarneros, and Rosemary Torres Lerma. Also contributing to the report were James Bennett, Holly Dye, Melissa Jaynes, Jill Lacey, Grant Mallie, Amanda Miller, Andrew Nelson, Heddi Nieuwsma, and Craig Winslow. |

# Related GAO Products

*Elder Justice, National Strategy Needed to Effectively Combat Elder Financial Exploitation.* GAO-13-110. Washington, D.C.: November 15, 2012.

*Elder Justice: Stronger Federal Leadership Could Enhance National Response to Elder Abuse.* GAO-11-208. Washington, D.C.: March 2, 2011.

*Older Americans Act: More Should Be Done to Measure the Extent of Unmet Need for Services.* GAO-11-237. Washington, D.C.: February 28, 2011.

| | |
|---|---|
| **GAO's Mission** | The Government Accountability Office, the audit, evaluation, and investigative arm of Congress, exists to support Congress in meeting its constitutional responsibilities and to help improve the performance and accountability of the federal government for the American people. GAO examines the use of public funds; evaluates federal programs and policies; and provides analyses, recommendations, and other assistance to help Congress make informed oversight, policy, and funding decisions. GAO's commitment to good government is reflected in its core values of accountability, integrity, and reliability. |
| **Obtaining Copies of GAO Reports and Testimony** | The fastest and easiest way to obtain copies of GAO documents at no cost is through GAO's website (http://www.gao.gov). Each weekday afternoon, GAO posts on its website newly released reports, testimony, and correspondence. To have GAO e-mail you a list of newly posted products, go to http://www.gao.gov and select "E-mail Updates." |
| **Order by Phone** | The price of each GAO publication reflects GAO's actual cost of production and distribution and depends on the number of pages in the publication and whether the publication is printed in color or black and white. Pricing and ordering information is posted on GAO's website, http://www.gao.gov/ordering.htm.<br><br>Place orders by calling (202) 512-6000, toll free (866) 801-7077, or TDD (202) 512-2537.<br><br>Orders may be paid for using American Express, Discover Card, MasterCard, Visa, check, or money order. Call for additional information. |
| **Connect with GAO** | Connect with GAO on Facebook, Flickr, Twitter, and YouTube. Subscribe to our RSS Feeds or E-mail Updates. Listen to our Podcasts. Visit GAO on the web at www.gao.gov. |
| **To Report Fraud, Waste, and Abuse in Federal Programs** | Contact:<br><br>Website: http://www.gao.gov/fraudnet/fraudnet.htm<br>E-mail: fraudnet@gao.gov<br>Automated answering system: (800) 424-5454 or (202) 512-7470 |
| **Congressional Relations** | Katherine Siggerud, Managing Director, siggerudk@gao.gov, (202) 512-4400, U.S. Government Accountability Office, 441 G Street NW, Room 7125, Washington, DC 20548 |
| **Public Affairs** | Chuck Young, Managing Director, youngc1@gao.gov, (202) 512-4800 U.S. Government Accountability Office, 441 G Street NW, Room 7149 Washington, DC 20548 |

Please Print on Recycled Paper.

www.ingramcontent.com/pod-product-compliance
Lightning Source LLC
Chambersburg PA
CBHW080543290526
45790CB00006B/2525